Banner Legacy

The Rise of the Fengtian Local Elite At the End of the Qing

Yoshiki Enatsu

Center for Chinese Studies
The University of Michigan
Ann Arbor

MICHIGAN MONOGRAPHS IN CHINESE STUDIES
ISSN 1081-9053
SERIES ESTABLISHED 1968
VOLUME 100

Published by
Center for Chinese Studies
The University of Michigan
Ann Arbor, Michigan 48104-1608

Library of Congress Cataloging-in-Publication Data

Enatsu, Yoshiki.
Banner legacy : the rise of the Fengtian local elite at the end of the Qing / Yoshiki Enatsu.
p. cm. – (Michigan monographs in Chinese studies ; 100)
Includes bibliographic references and index.
ISBN 0-89264-165-7 (alk. paper)
1. Manchus—China—Manchuria—History. 2. Manchuria (China)—History. 3. China—History—19th century. I. Title: Rise of the Fengtian elite at the end of the Qing. II. Title. III. Series.

DS731.M35E57 2004
95'.82033'08621—dc22

2004045745

ISBN: 978-1-938937-00-2 (paperback)

For Haruko

Contents

Illustrations

Maps

Tables

Acknowledgments

This work began as a doctoral dissertation at the University of Michigan in Ann Arbor. I am thankful to Professors Albert Feuerwerker and Ernest Young, who carefully read the draft chapter by chapter and gave me valuable advice on improving its contents. I was able to correct many mistakes in the earlier draft through consultation with both professors. Their comments also encouraged me to think about the meaning of this study from the broader viewpoint of modern Chinese history. I also wish to express my appreciation to Professors Rhoads Murphey and Robert Dernberger, who kindly commented on the contents of this study, the basic structure of the thesis, and English problems.

I am also indebted to Professors Manabu Nakagawa and Shigeru Ishikawa, whose helpful remarks on my earlier Japanese articles on the issue of modern Manchuria's land system fostered my pursuit of the study of modern Manchurian history.

I was able, at the Liaoning Provincial Archives in Shenyang and the First Historical Archives of China in Beijing, to add to the materials on which my dissertation was based. Financial aid provided by the Japanese Ministry of Education for the study of Manchurian history made it possible for me to do research at these Chinese archives. These projects were called "The Foundation of the Chinese World" and "Study of Historical Documents on the Formative Period of the Qing Dynasty." I am grateful to the head of the projects, Professor Yoshio Hosoya, and their members.

More than twelve years have passed since I finished my doctoral dissertation. Toward the completion of this book, Professor Ernest Young gave me new and valuable comments on the manuscript. Professor James Lee also steered me to recent studies on the banner people in Fengtian in the Qing period. Professor Noriko Kamachi has given continuous encouragement. I could not have finished this work without these professors' support.

I also wish to acknowledge the assistance of Nina Raj and Carol Yorkievitz with the revision of the manuscript.

September 2003
Ann Arbor, Michigan

Northern China circa 1908

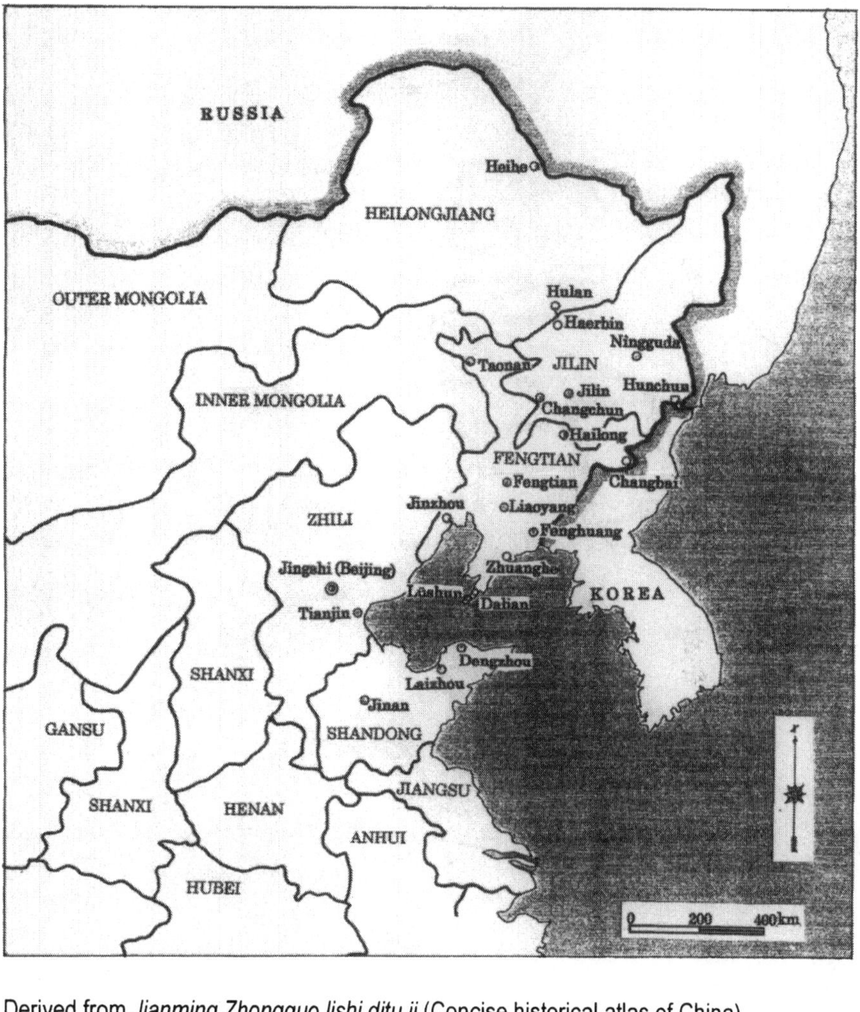

Derived from *Jianming Zhongguo lishi ditu ji* (Concise historical atlas of China) (Zhongguo ditu chubanshe, 1991), 67–68.

Liaoyang County circa 1908

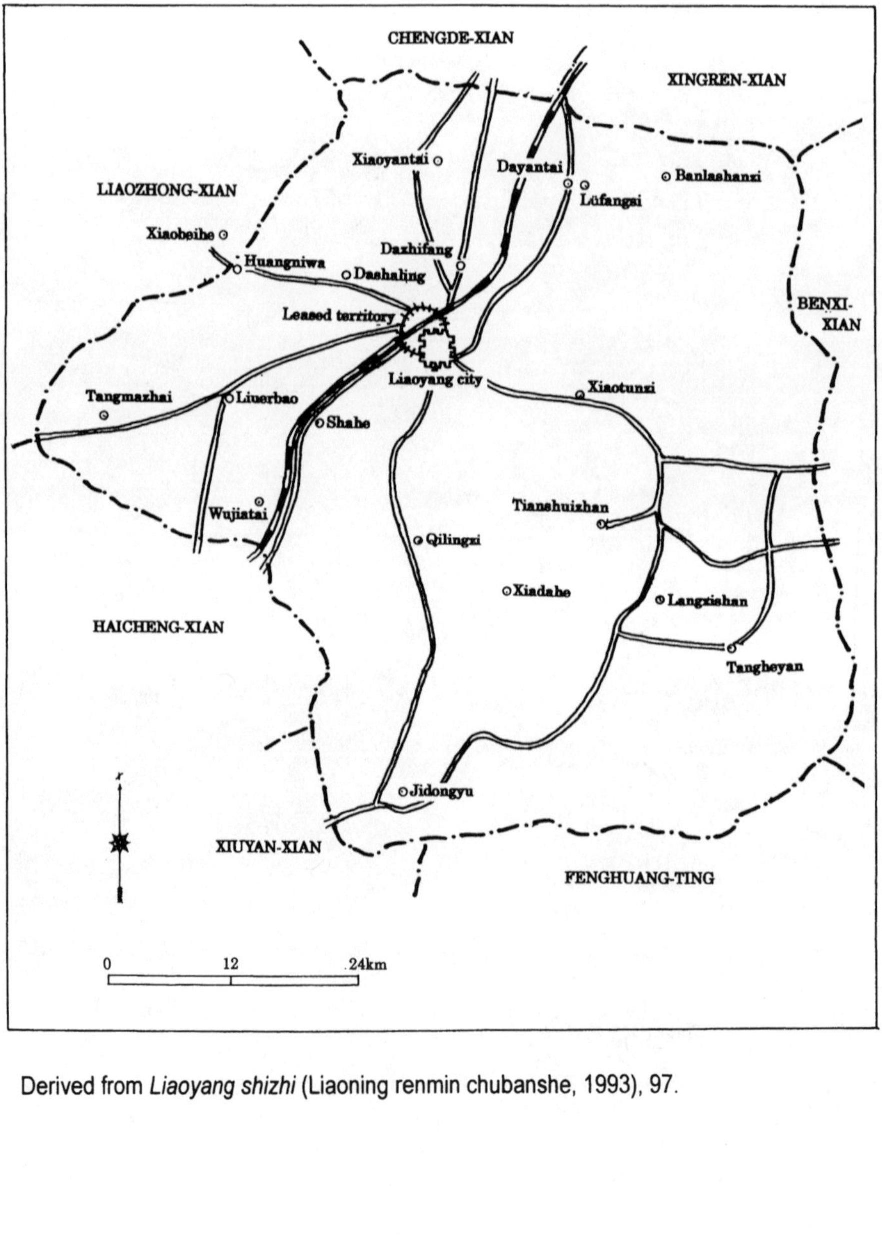

Derived from *Liaoyang shizhi* (Liaoning renmin chubanshe, 1993), 97.

Introduction

Manchuria, or China's Northeast (Dongbeibu), was called the Three Eastern Provinces (Dongsansheng) during the Qing and the early Republican periods. This vast area spreads north of Shanhaiguan at the easternmost end of the Great Wall and borders what is today Russia on the Amur (Heilong) River to the north, the Ussuri River to the east, and, separating it from the Korean peninsula, the Yalu and Tumen rivers to the south. To the west it adjoins the Mongol highlands. The Three Eastern Provinces were Fengtian, Jilin, and Heilongjiang; and Fengtian Province was also known as Shengjing until the beginning of the twentieth century. Through changes in administrative boundaries, the area that was the Three Eastern Provinces today constitutes not only the three provinces of Liaoning (formerly Fengtian), Jilin, and Heilongjiang, but also the eastern part of the Inner Mongolian Autonomous Region.

The Three Eastern Provinces came to be called Manchuria because they encompassed the homeland of the Manchu people.[1] The Manchus came from the southern part of this area in the latter half of the sixteenth century. They believed that they had descended from the Jurchen, whose homeland was also China's Northeast. The Jurchen founded the Jin dynasty (1115–1215) and ruled the northern part of China in the twelfth and thirteenth centuries. In 1616, the Manchus founded the Hou Jin (Later Jin) dynasty (1616–1636) and renamed it the Great Qing (1636–1912) in 1636. Qing armies entered China proper and established their capital in Beijing in 1644. Succeeding the Ming dynasty (1368–1644), the Qing ruled China until the beginning of the twentieth century.

From the end of the nineteenth century, Manchuria held a strategically important position in international politics. The Japanese army encroached upon southern Manchuria in 1894 at the time of the Sino-Japanese War, and the Russian army occupied all of Manchuria during the Boxer Rebellion of

1900. Japan successfully challenged Russia for control of this region in the 1904–1905 Russo-Japanese War, and continued to expand its influence there after the 1911 Revolution, including during the Zhang Zuolin regime (1916–1928). Japan finally conquered the whole area, establishing the puppet state Manzhouguo (1932–1945) in 1932, which at the time was referred to in English as Manchukuo. The international ramifications of Manchuria's situation involved not only the interests of China, Japan, and Russia/Soviet Union, but also those of Western countries such as the United States and the United Kingdom. The United Kingdom moved to check the spread of Russian power over Manchuria by entering into an alliance with Japan in 1902. During the first decade of the twentieth century, U.S. attempts to expand its influence in China took the form of American business and government efforts to extend railroad and business loans to Manchuria.

Manchuria's modern history was at first an integral part of Chinese history, but successive foreign invasions and Japanese aggression severely crippled Chinese sovereignty there, creating the context for a distinct Manchurian historical perspective. As groundwork for its effective control over the region, the Japanese government carried out systematic investigations of the actual conditions of Manchurian society. Its agents in these investigations were the South Manchuria Railroad Company (Minami Manshū Tetsudō Kabushiki Kaisha, or Mantetsu), the Japanese colonial authority of the Guandong Leased Territory (Kantō-chō), and the Manzhouguo (Manshūkoku) government. These agencies produced a vast number of research documents, a rich storehouse of information about Manchurian society under Japanese influence and eventual control, spanning the turn of the century through 1945.[2]

These documents have allowed researchers to examine a range of topics concerning Manchurian politics, economy, and society in the first half of the twentieth century.[3] But often these studies have not treated the area as an integral part of modern Chinese history. Because their foci have generally been issues related to Japan's invasion and control of Manchuria, they have not paid much attention to Manchurian society prior to the Japanese invasion, and therefore, have basically limited their analysis to Japanese documents. Although these studies occasionally report large-scale Han Chinese immigration from China proper to Manchuria and point to the area's rapid agricultural development from the mid-nineteenth century on, they usually characterize Manchuria as a frontier wasteland before the Japanese invasion, examining only those features that established it as a newly developed area. This picture, however, is incorrect. Southern Manchuria was already a well-developed agricultural area in the Ming period, and a rich agrarian society thrived there throughout the Qing.

Numerous studies have been done of early seventeenth-century Manchurian history. Documents recorded in Manchu and Chinese, such as *Manwen laodang* (Secret chronicles of the Manchu dynasty), describe how Nurhaci (1559–1626) and Hong Taiji (1592–1643) unified the Manchu people and established a centralized dynasty before claiming Beijing as their capital in the seventeenth century.[4] Their interest, however, lies mainly in the history of the Manchu dynasty and its people, and not necessarily in that of Manchuria per se. Because such a large number of Manchus moved into China proper after the establishment of the Qing, for most, their original homeland had come to seem a relatively remote area.

We therefore have limited knowledge of Manchurian society during the Qing period, although some studies of the region's history in that era do exist. For example, the historical surveys of Manchurian society written by Inaba Iwakichi and Sudō Yoshiyuki help us understand such distinct features as the Qing policy of *Manzhou fengjin,* which prohibited Han Chinese from immigrating into Manchuria from the beginning of the eighteenth century through the mid-nineteenth century, the growth of Chinese settlements in Manchuria from the mid-nineteenth century, and changes in the administrative system of Manchuria over the course of the Qing.[5] Based upon the accomplishments of these pre-war studies, Robert Lee and Chao Chung-fu have deepened our understanding of Manchuria's history, emphasizing how Manchurian society had became increasingly sinicized through the expansion of the Han Chinese population from the mid-Qing period on.[6] In another noteworthy study, Thomas Gottschang and Diana Lary present research on the immigration patterns of Han people from China proper to Manchuria in the modern era and analyze the economic and social mechanisms of that immigration.[7]

Partly because of the dearth of historical documents, we still have only limited knowledge about the realities of Manchurian society itself during the Qing. But we cannot grasp the real nature of modern Manchuria's history without analyzing its Qing era society. For example, some of the problems that confronted the Zhang Zuolin regime and the Japanese puppet state of

Manzhouguo were historically constituted in the very fabric of Manchurian society. In other words, these governments were faced with issues deeply rooted in the social structure inherited from the Qing period. The subject of this study then—the complicated relations between Manchuria's local elites and the government authorities sent by the Qing court—was one of those problems.

★ ★ ★

The common view that Manchuria was a frontier region prior to the 1911 Revolution is simplistic. Yet in the study of modern Chinese history, with its focus on "waves of revolution," this area has always been considered "politically backward." Indeed, at the time of the 1911 Revolution, the Three Eastern Provinces were unable to achieve their independence from the Qing dynasty while many other provinces did. Even after the 1911 Revolution and the establishment of the Republic (1912–), Zhao Erxun (1844–1927), the former Qing-appointed governor-general (*zongdu*) of the Three Eastern Provinces, stayed on as governor (*dudu*) of Fengtian Province, thus seeming to maintain the old Qing system. But were the social and political systems of Manchuria at the end of the Qing period really old? To answer this question, we must examine when and how the regime or administrative system of Manchuria, as it existed at the time of the 1911 Revolution, was established.

Manchurian society experienced an important transformation through the reform programs implemented by the Qing during the first decade of the twentieth century. In a nationwide movement calling for the drafting of a constitution and establishment of a parliament, these progressive efforts sought changes in the existing administrative and political systems. We call these reforms at the close of the Qing period the New Policies. Within the framework of the New Policies, for example, were such initiatives as the abolition of the traditional civil service examinations, the establishment of a new school system, the foundation of new police and judicial institutions, and the inauguration of self-governing organizations in local communities. One key project of the reform was the Qing government's establishment of provincial assemblies (*ziyiju*), with the expectation that leading local figures would be elected to the provincial assemblies and collaborate with their centrally appointed provincial administrators. Simply put, the basic strategy of the Qing government was to reconstruct its effective control over local society.

Within Manchuria, the most progressive reform programs were conducted in Fengtian, the southernmost province and the center of Manchuria's politics and economy. In an attempt to prohibit Han Chinese from emigrating from China proper, the Qing dynasty had placed Manchuria, homeland of the Manchus, under military control until the first decade of the twentieth century, while the provinces in China proper were controlled by civil administration. Military governors (*jiangjun*) appointed from among high-ranking officials belonging to the Eight Banners (*baqi*) governed the three administrative districts of Fengtian (Shengjing), Jilin, and Heilongjiang. With the exception of a limited number of civil offices (*min yamen*), the banner offices (*qi yamen*) under these generals controlled the people and land in Manchuria.

After the Russo-Japanese War, the Qing government changed the administrative system of the region from a military to a civil one, a move by which it proclaimed its view that Manchuria was an indivisible part of China. In 1907 Xu Shichang (1855–1939), an intimate associate of Yuan Shikai (1859–1916), who became president of the Republic after the 1911 Revolution, was dispatched to Fengtian as the first governor-general of the Three Eastern Provinces. Xiliang (1853–1917), a famous reform-minded official and Mongol bannerman, succeeded him two years later in 1909.[8] Under the Xu Shichang and Xiliang administrations, local offices of the civil administration (*zhou*, *xian*, and *ting*) were expanded, and their officials carried out extensive reform programs. The regime in Manchuria at the time of the 1911 Revolution, commonly considered "old," was in fact based on a relatively new power structure. This being the case, modern Manchurian history cannot be understood without studying the reform programs implemented by the Qing government at the beginning of the twentieth century.

There were two important consequences of the reform programs in Fengtian. The first was the rise of local power. If we compare the political system of Fengtian Province before and after the 1911 Revolution in terms of the power of local elites, we find a radical change. From the time of the 1911 Revolution, actual power in the provincial administration began to shift from the hands of bureaucrats sent by the central government to those of powerful local figures. Local power holders continued to wield strong influence in the world of Manchurian politics until the fall of Manzhouguo in 1945. Therefore, how these local elites secured their positions in Fengtian society at the beginning of the twentieth century and then began to assume control of provincial politics is of great interest in the study of modern Manchurian history.

The second consequence of the reform program was the dismantling of the system of banner land (*qidi*) and official land (*guandi*). Until almost the end of the dynasty, a large portion of the land in Fengtian was organized as banner land and official land under the Eight Banner system.[9] This land was reserved as a possession of the Qing court, its nobles, and its bannermen. The Qing court in particular controlled a vast area. Under the administration of court offices such as the Neiwufu (Imperial Household Department), these lands were primarily managed and tilled by Han peasants enrolled in the banner system. Many of these Han bannermen sublet such land to Han Chinese peasants. From the middle of the Qing period, actual control of the land increasingly fell into the hands of powerful Han bannermen who acted as managers of the manors.

The Qing government's reorganization of official and banner lands into civil land was one of the key reform programs in Fengtian. The government realized that these lands could no longer function for the sole economic benefit of the court and the Manchu people. The Fengtian provincial government under the Qing therefore sold vast areas of the land to private civilians, placing former official and banner land under civil jurisdiction. Through these sales, the Fengtian provincial government could obtain the financial resources necessary to implement the New Policies. The provincial government needed an enormous amount of money to set up new police and judicial institutions, establish local self-governing organizations, and so forth. The men who already had *defacto* control of the land, such as managers of the Qing manors, were generally granted a first option to buy the land that they had administered. In this way official and banner land in Fengtian began to rapidly disappear through the land reform program.

The consequences of the reforms in Fengtian were two sides of the same coin: It is highly likely that some powerful Han bannermen purchased or simply occupied the official lands they had originally controlled under the banner system. As new landlords, they were perfectly positioned to become the core of a local elite in Fengtian. This work will address the process of their advance to political power.

* * *

This discussion must begin with the institution of the Han banners. Many prominent Fengtian leaders were Han bannermen (*Hanjun qiren*) who became politically active in the turmoil leading up to the 1911 Revolution and the fall of the Qing. Zhao Erxun, Zhang Rong (1884–1912), and Yuan Jinkai (1869–1947) were among them. Zhao Erxun was the governor-general of the Three Eastern Provinces during that revolution. Zhang Rong was a leader of the anti-Qing movement there, while Yuan Jinkai was a leading local figure at that time who helped Zhao Erxun. Why was it that Han bannermen assumed such prominent roles? What are the origins and the history of Han bannermen and what did it mean to be one? As we consider these questions, we will also explore the historical background of the Fengtian local elite.

The second chapter will examine the specific characteristics of the Fengtian local elite in terms of the land system. Much of Fengtian was classified as official and banner land during the Qing period, and civilians were prohibited from owning it. Logically, official land did not have landowners. Yet by the end of the Qing period many Han bannermen, who did in fact function as landowners, controlled a large part of formerly official land. This chapter investigates the disposition of official land conducted by the Xu Shichang and Xiliang administrations of the Fengtian provincial government. How did certain Han bannermen acquire ownership of official land and establish an economic base as landlords? And how did they achieve their subsequent success as local elites?

Chapter 3 will explain how the local elite of Fengtian, including many Han bannermen, was mobilized in support of the provincial government. After the Russian occupation following on the Boxer Rebellion and the Russian and Japanese occupations at the time of the Russo-Japanese War, the Fengtian provincial government had lost effective control over its people and land. Therefore, an important task for the provincial government beginning in 1905 was to re-establish that control. It sought the support of local elites in order to do so and integrated them into its administrative system under such self-governing institutions as provincial assemblies. By looking at the actual process of the elections to the Fengtian Provincial Assembly, I will suggest how the local elite collaborated and began to pursue their interests in provincial politics. Certain important actors emerged as leaders of the self-governing institutions and formed the core of later Fengtian provincial bureaucracies. They continued as powerful players until the fall of Manzhouguo.

The fourth chapter will consider the personal history of Yuan Jinkai and other members of the local elite in Fengtian's Liaoyang County. Yuan was originally a leader of the local militia in Liaoyang at the time of the Boxer Rebellion and the Russo-Japanese War. He later headed the Fengtian police system and was elected to the Provincial Assembly. He was the right-hand man to Zhao Erxun, the governor-general of the Three Eastern Provinces at the time of the 1911 Revolution, and later served in both the Zhang Zuolin regime and the Manzhouguo government. The case histories of Yuan Jinkai and other local elites effectively illustrate how local leaders in Fengtian gained power in provincial politics through the reform programs of the Qing government in the early twentieth century.

In chapter 5 we will investigate the 1911 Revolution in Fengtian. After the uprising of the New Army in Wuchang, the anti-Qing movement spread quickly to Fengtian and pushed the provincial administration of the Qing government to the verge of collapse. The governor-general of the Three Eastern Provinces asked provincial leaders to help its administration suppress the revolutionary movement. Thereafter, mobilized by Yuan Jinkai, local leaders moved in to control provincial politics, taking over posts formerly held by the Qing officials.

★ ★ ★

This is a case study of Chinese local elites in a peripheral zone. Much literature on modern China examines how local elites acquired formal political positions when the central bureaucratic power of the imperial state declined beginning in the mid-nineteenth century. They stress that flexible reliance on multiple resources such as military power, education, land, commerce, lineage organizations, and personal networks was an important characteristic of the local elite of the day.[10] The Fengtian local elite also rose to power through the mobilization of similar resources. Their acquisition of military power is especially worth examining.

Philip Kuhn has studied local militarization in South and Central China in the 1850's where the power of the Qing government weakened during the turmoil of the Taiping Rebellion. Kuhn's monograph on this topic examines how elites gained power through the process of local militarization and scrutinizes their relation to the state bureaucracy.[11] In Manchuria, it was at the beginning of the twentieth century when many members of the local elite augmented their social power by gaining control of the local militia and began to acquire access to provincial officialdom. Even though the period and the area of investigation are different, Kuhn's study of local militarization is full of implications for this study. In twentieth-century Manchuria, too, local militarization and the grasp of official power by the local elite should be key topics in the study of its modern history.

There are already a number of monographs about the rise of the local elite in several provinces during the last half century of the Qing period. For example, Mary Rankin and Joseph Esherick have studied elite political activity in Zhejiang Province, and Hunan and Hubei provinces, respectively.[12] Their work investigates how the local elites became deeply engaged in political activities as part of the Qing's reform programs. The present study will illustrate how the local elite in Fengtian organized the same kind of political movements at the time of the New Policies. Indeed, the case of Fengtian's local elites gives us a close view of how the centralized power structure of the Qing deteriorated at the local level and how a local elite emerged through the process of implementing the New Policies.

At the same time, however, some sources of power among Fengtian's local elites were very different from those in other areas of China proper. In Fengtian's case, the acquisition of official and banner lands and the social networks of the Han bannermen community were important resources. These resources were drawn from the particular conditions and history of Manchuria, a region administered during the Qing period through the Eight Banner system. In other words, the Fengtian local elite emerged as a new power by using, to some degree, the existing social structure. But, like elsewhere, the push of the reforms, especially the disposition of the official lands and the establishment of self-governing organizations, also contributed to their emergence.

While the beginning of this book briefly presents a history of the banners and their land system in Manchuria, the book's main discussion, chapters 3 through 5, will specifically examine the rise of the Fengtian local elite at the end of the Qing period. As mentioned above, to grasp the historical progress of Fengtian's local elites, it is important to examine their family backgrounds, that is to say, their situation within the Qing banner system. These elites, many of whom were Han bannermen, emerged from the dismantled banner system, and it is important to understand just how the collapse of that system helped them to acquire power.

For my discussion of the banner system, I rely upon the core Japanese studies such as *Manshū kyūkan chōsa hōkoku-sho* by Amagai Kenzaburō and those by Sudō Yoshiyuki and Ura Ren'ichirō.[13] These studies, although conducted in the pre-war period, are still considered basic works in the field, and a fresh reconsideration of them is in order. The *Manshū kyūkan chōsa hōkoku-sho* is a prime example. It explains the banners and their land system in Manchuria by focusing upon the manor system of the Qing court offices. Although they consider the manors of such key offices as the Neiwufu (Imperial Household Department) and the Shengjing hubu (Board of Revenue in Shengjing), they do not pay much attention to manor lands owned by Qing nobles or the banner lands possessed by Qing bannermen. But such lands extended over huge areas throughout Manchuria in the Qing period. We still have only limited knowledge about these extensive holdings, though a more complete picture of the banner system and its lands in Manchuria must surely take them into account. In short, the world covered in the classic Japanese works on Manchuria is only part of the picture.

In addition, the explanation given in these studies of the status of Han people enrolled in the banner system is questionable. Amagai and other scholars assumed that these Han banner people were treated less favorably within the banner system. But according to more recent studies by James Lee and other scholars, those Han banner people in fact belonged to the elite "Upper Three Banners," which fell under the direct control of the emperor, and enjoyed full status as bannermen. Some of the leading figures in the Fengtian local elite were enrolled in these units in the Qing period, and it was natural that they should attain power because of their privileged status in the banner system. On the other hand, we have very limited information about Han banner people who were organized outside the Upper Three Banners, such as subordinates on the Qing nobles' manors. This raises some basic questions. What was the difference between Han banner people in Manchuria who belonged to the Upper Three Banners and those who did not? Did status differences exist among the Han people who held positions under the Upper Three Banners? To get a more concrete picture of the banner system in Manchuria, we need to do further study of the status of Han banner people there.

The Fengtian local elite emerged through the collapse of the banner system at the end of the Qing period. While the government in Manchuria changed hands several times after the Qing, certain leading figures of the local elite continued to occupy key official positions for decades. Therefore, by focusing our research on the movements of the Fengtian local elite, it is possible to discuss the history of the province as a continuous flow—from the close of the Qing period, through the 1911 Revolution and the Zhang Zuolin government, to the Manzhouguo period—rather than as separate topics, as has been done previously. By examining the rise of the Fengtian local elite in provincial politics at the end of the Qing period and following its transition into the post-1911 Republic, this study will address aspects of southern Manchurian society upon which earlier studies have not yet touched.

CHAPTER 1

Han Bannermen Society in Qing Period Fengtian

The Eight Banner System

The Manchu people, originally called Jurchen, lived in Manchuria, and at the close of the Ming period they consisted of three tribal groups: the Jianzhou, the Haixi, and the Yeren. Banners are believed to have originally been units organized for large-scale hunts among the Jurchen. Nurhaci, a Jianzhou leader, reorganized these hunting units into banners for warfare. In the late Ming period, the Jianzhou tribe lived in the Suzi River basin of southern Manchuria, while the Haixi tribe was settled north of the Jianzhou and Yeren tribes in the northeastern outskirts of Manchuria. Mobilizing the banner system, Nurhaci unified the Jurchen people and founded the Later Jin dynasty. Hong Taiji, Nurhaci's son, succeeded him as khan in 1626, and renamed the dynasty the Great Qing in 1636.[1]

Ignoring tribal origins, Nurhaci reorganized the banners as military, bureaucratic, and social units based upon family affiliations. The basic unit within the banners (*gusa*) was the company (*niru*). One banner was composed of twenty-five companies. All Manchus belonged to a banner and were placed under the control and protection of the banner in which they were enrolled. They were regulated administratively, taxed, and mobilized through their banners. Banners and their component companies contributed a specified quota of men to make up needed military forces. It is said that the head (*ejen*) of each banner originally commanded about 7,500 soldiers, although in actuality, the number of companies in each banner was not necessarily twenty-five, and the size of each company differed as well. As a result, some banners retained more than 7,500 soldiers, and some had fewer. In the process of unification of the Jurchen by Nurhaci and Hong Taiji, the Haixi and the Yeren tribes were integrated into the banner system. Nurhaci first founded a system with four banners in 1601 and expanded it into the Eight Banner system in 1614. These eight banners were named after the pattern of color on the banner that represented each unit: Bordered Yellow (*xianghuang*), Plain Yellow (*zhenghuang*), Plain White (*zhengbai*), Bordered White (*xiangbai*), Plain Red (*zhenghong*), Bordered Red (*xianghong*), Plain Blue (*zhenglan*), and Bordered Blue (*xianglan*).[2]

The Eight Banner system initially included only Manchus, but Hong Taiji established attached Mongolian and Han banners in 1635 and 1642. When the Later Jin had conquered southern and western Manchuria, it began to govern a large number of Han Chinese and Mongols.[3] These Mongols and Han, enrolled in the banner system, would play a significant role in the Qing conquest of China. Through a process of organizational enlargement, the Han banner system actually took shape in the Shunzhi (1644–1661) and Kangxi (1662–1722) periods, after the establishment of the Qing dynasty in Beijing. Compared to the pre-Qing history of the Eight Banners, we have limited detailed knowledge of how the system functioned after 1644, the year the Manchus entered China proper. One widely held view is that the Qing dynasty was soon sinicized, especially after the Yongzheng period (1723–1735), and that a Han-style bureaucratic system dominated the Qing administration. This approach emphasizes the continuity of Ming features in the Qing dynasty but pays little attention to the role of the Eight Banner system.

An opposing school of thought argues that the Qing state not only retained its Manchu features after the Yongzheng period, but the Eight Banner system also functioned throughout as a key institution in the Manchu control of China. The Manchu armies, organized in banner garrisons, were stationed in Beijing and in other strategically important cities and areas. These garrisons were the domiciles of Manchu officers, soldiers, and their families. In fact, they lived inside banner boundaries within special districts designated for Manchus in Beijing and in other cities. The Qing protected the structure of banner society until the dynasty's collapse in 1911. Therefore, scholars of this school of thought regard inquiry into the Eight Banner system as key to the study of Qing history.

Recently, Chinese and Japanese students as well as Anglophone scholars have paid more attention to the Eight Banner system. For example, there is

Pamela Crossley's history of a Manchu bannerman family, the Guwalgiya family,[4] and Mark Elliott's examination of various dimensions of the Manchu world and the crisis of bannerman self-identity as it became assimilated to Han culture.[5] Edward Rhoads has delved into Manchu-Han relations at the end of the Qing period in his discussion of how Cixi and Zaifeng, dominant figures in the court, dealt with this issue.[6]

In spite of recent progress in the study of the Eight Banner system, however, certain important subjects have yet to be examined. For example, we know very little about the system underlying the Mongolian and Han banners. For this book, research into the history of Han bannermen is significant because so many of them lived in Fengtian in the Qing period, and some would play a major role in the modern history of Manchuria.

The Population of Han Bannermen in Fengtian Province

It is rather surprising how large the population of Han bannermen actually was in Fengtian Province during the Qing. In a 1908 investigation by the Fengtian Provincial Assembly, cited in *Manshū chihō-shi* (Compilation of surveys conducted by Japan's Governor-general's Office in Lüshun, Kantō Totoku-fu), 1,823,359 persons (17.8 percent) out of the total registered population of 10,238,309 in Fengtian Province were classified as Han bannermen (*Hanjun*), and most of these were engaged in agriculture. Further, Han bannermen made up 21.2 percent of the total Han population (8,585,154) in the province (Table 1). According to the same report, in Fengtianfu, a prefectural subdivision of Fengtian Province, 68,865 (76.1 percent) out of a registered 90,409 Han bannermen were peasants.

These figures reveal that Fengtian's large Han bannermen population in the late Qing constituted an identifiable community within this region. Many of them lived in fertile areas in the Liaodong plain, a well-developed agricultural region in southern Manchuria. In fact, the population of bannermen was greater than that of ordinary Han people (*Hanren*) in Liaoyang County, and it appears that a large proportion of bannermen were effectively part of the general population, though some of them enjoyed special privileges as members of the banner system.[7]

Manshū chihō-shi uses the expression "Han bannermen" (*Hanjun*) to refer to Han people who, although evidently not military by profession, were registered in the banner system, including women and children. To specify this particular subgroup, we may call them banner people (*qiren*) of Han ethnicity. On the other hand, in the study of Qing history, the term "Han bannermen" generally indicates members of a primarily military caste who were registered in the Han Banners (*Baqi Hanjun*). As a privileged class of the Qing dynasty, they were granted full status as bannermen. We may call them regular Han bannermen.

Table 1. Households and Population of Fengtian Province, 1908

	Number of Households	Population
Manchus	78,067	485,959
Mongols	23,422	161,292
Han Chinese	1.045,726	6,761,795
Muslim Chinese	6,742	38,739
Han Bannermen	290,988	1,823,359
Sojourners	136,084	918,917
Foreigners	12,026	48,248
Total	1.593,055	10,238,309

Source: Kantō Totoku-fu, ed., *Manshū chihō-shi*, 1911, vol. 1, 12.

This raises some questions. Why did so many Han people living in Fengtian Province enroll in the banner system? What kind of banner people were they? Was there any difference in status within the banner system between regular Han bannermen and the many other people of Han ethnicity who were registered in the banners in Fengtian?

A description in the work *Guochao jianye chuji jilüe* (Brief history on the first basis for the foundation of the dynasty) gives us valuable information about those Han banner people who lived in Fengtian. This document, compiled by the Neiwufu (Imperial Household Department) in 1894, explains the basic structure of the administrative system in Shengjing (the subsidiary Qing capital for Manchuria) and its regulations during the Qing period. According to this source, the Neiwufu in Shengjing controlled a vast area of land and the peasants who lived there. These peasants were obliged to pay a small amount of cash and provide agricultural and other products to the Neiwufu. A large number supplied mainly grains, but some were engaged in the production of salt, indigo, cotton, and other products. The *Guochao jianye chuji jilüe* explains that in 1893 more than 139,900 Han banner people belonged to the office of the Neiwufu and to the Upper Three Banners (*shangsanqi*—the Bordered Yellow, Plain Yellow, and Plain White banners) of the Shengjing Neiwufu. These bannermen were for the most part engaged in cultivation.[8]

In his capacity as investigator for the South Manchurian Railroad Company, Amagai Kenzaburō inquired into the landholding structure of Manchuria at the beginning of the twentieth century. His reports, *Naimufu Kanshō* (Manors of the Imperial Household Department) and *Kōsan* (Lands owned by the Qing court), explain that many of these peasants lived on manors owned by court offices. They also indicate that a large number of Han males were registered in the Upper Three Banners and belonged to the Neiwufu, the Shengjing Board of Revenue (*hubu*), Board of Rites (*libu*), and Board of Works (*gongbu*), as well as the Sanling ("the three tombs" of Nurhaci, Hong Taiji, and their ancestors). Many of them were peasants and their basic duty was to cultivate manor lands and to supply agricultural and other products to Qing court offices such as the Neiwufu. Amagai examined the manor system in Fengtian at the end of the Qing period in great detail. He emphasized that there was a large group of Han people registered under the banner system in Fengtian Province and that their status in that system was different from that of regular Han bannermen. Amagai called them "banner males on official manors" (*guanzhuang qiding*).[9]

It is generally held that the Qing treated these Han banner people of the Neiwufu less favorably than regular Han bannermmen. Wang Zhonghan, a leading Chinese scholar in this field, explains that they had inferior status in such areas as eligibility for the civil service examinations, inclusion in military mobilization, receipt of pensions, pardon from punishment, and so forth.[10] It is, however, also true that their status was not necessarily clear even to Qing officials. For example, in 1891, Yu Lu, military governor of Shengjing, and Ting Mao, the magistrate of Fengtian prefecture, specifically reported to the throne that the managers and tillers of the Neiwufu manors were both eligible to take the civil service examinations and to buy banner land, indicating some fluidity in their status within the banner system. Yu and Ting concluded that these Han banner people of the Neiwufu had the same status as regular bannermen, that is to say, *zhengshen qiren* (bannermen with full status).[11] As suggested in the introduction, we need further investigation into the status of Han banner people who belonged to court offices such as the Neiwufu and those belonging to the banners as a whole to better understand the operation of distinctions between them.

At the end of the Qing period, Han people in the banner system in Fengtian, such as the subordinates of the Neiwufu, referred to themselves as Han bannermen (*Hanjun*). Other people in those days also regarded them as Han bannermen, as did a 1908 survey taken by the Fengtian Provincial Assembly. As a result, it is difficult to distinguish them from regular Han bannermen in the study of modern Manchurian history. For the purposes of this book, we will simply refer to all banner personnel as "Han bannermen" except in cases where there is a need to specify that they were Han people in the banner system, but not regular Han bannermen.

Because the Han people in the banner system made up a considerable part of the Han population in Fengtian Province, the investigation of their society has become one of the main subjects in the study of modern Manchurian history. James Lee and Cameron Campbell have examined the society of Han people in Fengtian's banner system from the viewpoint of demographic history by analyzing birth, marriage, death, and social success.[12] Ding Yizhuang, Guo Songyi, James Lee, and Cameron Campbell are also in the process of investigating family histories by examining the family registers of banner households (*hukouce*) and family records (*jiapu*), and by interviewing their descendants.[13] Gaining a more concrete understanding of how Han people in the banner system in Fengtian came to be enrolled in their banners and how they functioned within the system in the Qing period will be crucial to our later discussion of how some of their descendants played a key role in Fengtian politics at the end of the Qing.

Origins of the Han Bannermen

Although until recently Western historians have paid little attention to Han bannermen, Ura Ren'ichirō, Sudō Yoshiyuki, and Amagai Kenzaburō decades ago initiated investigations into their origins and their position in Chinese society during the Qing. Even though these studies are now somewhat out of date, they still provide a good place to begin.[14]

According to Ura and Sudō, two large groups of Han Chinese were enrolled in banners. The first was comprised of former officials and soldiers of the Ming army and their descendants. These officials originally defended the Liaodong area of southern Manchuria from Manchu conquest and then surrendered with their subordinate soldiers to the Manchu dynasty prior to the Qing advance into China proper. They and their descendants were eventually organized into Han banners. Surviving soldiers led by Shang Kexi (1604–1676) and Geng Zhongming (?–1671), for example, were so reorganized after the Rebellion of the Three Feudatories (1673–1681).[15]

A second type of Han bannermen consisted of ordinary Liaodong peasants. When the Manchus conquered Liaodong in the early seventeenth century, many Han Chinese landowners and peasants surrendered themselves and their lands to Manchu princes, nobles, and high-ranking officers in an act called *daidi touchong* (the surrender of oneself with one's land to the conqueror).[16] An especially large number of landowners and peasants surrendered to the Qing in Liaoyang and Shenyang districts, highly developed agricultural areas of Liaodong. These Liaodong peasants were often enrolled in banners when the Qing reorganized the surrendered lands into banner lands and various types of manors. These peasants were usually permitted to manage and cultivate the land they had surrendered as long as they paid annual rents to the Qing court and its nobles.[17] These two types of Han bannermen, former Ming officials and soldiers and Liaodong peasants, were placed under the control and protection of the Qing banners in which they were enrolled.

According to Ura, in addition to the act of "surrendering oneself with one's land to the conqueror," Han Chinese soldiers and peasants in the Liaodong area were also occasionally enrolled in Manchu banners as a result of capture by the Manchu armies. Such Han Chinese were registered as banner people but they were called *booi*, which means "bondservant" in

Manchu.[18] The Qing government in fact did treat this group less favorably than regular Han bannermen in such areas as eligibility for the civil service examinations.[19] In the evolution of the banner system, members of the Manchu banners included not only Manchus but also Han Chinese, Mongolians, Koreans, and Russians. While some Han in the Manchu banners were later reregistered under the Han banners, some would remain in the Manchu banners as *booi*. Thus the Eight Banners were not necessarily organized only along ethnic lines. Later *booi* were also called "Han bannermen," but in the broad sense, meaning they were the banner people of Han ethnicity.

Ura, Sudō, and Amagai's explanations give us a basic understanding of the origins of Han bannermen. But in addition, according to ongoing studies by James Lee and other scholars mentioned above, one additional and essential source of Han people enrolled in the banner system in Fengtian has been determined. This was immigration from China proper, mainly from Shandong Province.[20] At the beginning of the Qing period, the government encouraged Han people to immigrate to Manchuria (*Manzhou zhaomin kaikenli*). However, by the early eighteenth century, the settlement of Han people there had been banned (*Manzhou fengjin*), as the Qing tried to reserve Manchu land for Manchu bannermen. In spite of this policy, a huge number of peasants from China proper immigrated to southern Manchuria in search of new lands for cultivation,

Beginning in the late seventeenth century, a large number of these immigrants were organized into the banner system and many of them were engaged in cultivation of banner lands and manor land, such as that of the Neiwufu. These immigrants and their descendants greatly increased the number of Han people in Fengtian, and recent studies contend that they made up a considerable part of the Han banner population there.

There were two reasons why the Manchu dynasty organized so many Han people in the banner system. First, they needed Han Chinese military power. The Manchu dynasty was weak in numbers when it faced the Ming armies in Liaodong in the first half of the seventeenth century. In 1615 Manchu soldiers are said to have numbered only about 60,000.[21] It would have been impossible for the Manchus to conquer China by themselves, and therefore the Later Jin was eager to win Han Chinese soldiers over to their side. *Manwen laodang* includes frequent passages illustrating how the Manchus richly rewarded surrendering Ming officials and soldiers with silver and titles of honor. The following description is one of many examples:

> The twenty-seventh day of the fifth month in the first year of Chongde [1636]: The Taizong Emperor held a grand party for the former Ming officials Kong Youde, Shang Kexi, and Geng Zhongming, who had surrendered to the Manchu dynasty. The Emperor rewarded them with silver for their meritorious deeds. In addition, these three officials were given the titles King of Gongshun, King of Huaishun, and King of Zhishun, respectively.[22]

The Manchus also took great interest in the Ming armies' heavy weapons. Ura's study particularly emphasizes this point. Cannons called *hongyi pao*, literally "cannons of the red-faced barbarian," were imported from Portugal and guaranteed Ming military superiority over the Manchus. Nurhaci himself died from a wound from a Ming cannonball in Ningyuan, Liaodong. Besides welcoming Ming officials and soldiers who were armed with cannons, the Manchus favored artisans who could produce heavy weapons. Han Chinese were known for their ability to handle cannons installed on ships. Indeed, the original Manchu name for Han bannermen was *ujen cooha*, which means "heavy army," an expression that clearly illustrates the original defining feature of these forces.[23]

The second reason the Manchus organized Han banners was their usefulness in establishing a base from which to generate wealth for members and offices within the Qing regime. As described earlier, the Qing dynasty assigned various parcels of land all across Manchuria. These lands, later classified as official and banner lands, included Manchu bannermen's land, the manors of Manchu nobles, and the manors of court offices. In the early Qing period these lands were meant to provide an economic foundation for the Manchus, and Han Chinese were strictly prohibited from owning them.[24] When the dynasty decided to enroll Han peasants and immigrants into the Liaodong area banners, it had a special purpose in mind. The Han were skilled farmers and the Qing expected these new bannermen to manage and till official lands.[25]

An additional group of Han bannermen was engaged in the cultivation of manor lands. After the pacification of China proper, many former Ming soldiers who had helped the Qing conquer China were disarmed and sent back to Fengtian, their homeland. There they served the Qing dynasty as agricultural laborers rather than soldiers. Many of them had been subordinates of Wu Sangui (1612–1678), Shang Kexi, and Geng Jimao (?–1671), former Ming officials granted the title of prince for their meritorious deeds during the Qing conquest. After the establishment of the Qing dynasty in Beijing in 1644, these three princes were allowed to have their own kingdoms in Yunnan, Guangdong, and Fujian, respectively. When the Qing rulers tried to establish a centralized government, the three princes, headed by Wu Sangui, had rebelled in 1673, but the Qing government suppressed the rebellion in 1681. Afterward, their subordinates were returned to their homes in southern Manchuria, where they and their descendants were placed under the jurisdiction of banner offices in Fengtian. These became the ancestors of the Han bannermen Ura refers to as the surviving soldiers led by Shang Kexi and Geng Zhongming.[26] Many of them were now obliged to become managers (*zhuangtou*) and tillers (*zhuangding*) of the newly founded manors, a livelihood that became hereditary for their descendants.

An interview conducted in 1937 by Amagai Kenzaburō, when he was a member of the research staff in the Manzhouguo government, provides a good example of this. In it a former Han bannerman, Ling Yunge, manager of one of the Neiwufu manors in Suizhong prefecture during the Qing, explained that his ancestor had been a Ming soldier under Kong Youde. The post of manor manager was bestowed upon Ling's ancestor for his meritorious service.[27] We will discuss Ling family's history in more detail in the next chapter.

With the integration of these disarmed soldiers and immigrants from China proper into the banner system, the population of Han bannermen in Fengtian grew rapidly indeed after the close of the seventeenth century.

The Dual Identity of Han Bannermen

The ruling ethnic group of the Qing dynasty was Manchu. However, Han bannermen were also regarded as members of the Manchu system, and as bannermen, they were given special protections by the Qing. They were not placed under the jurisdiction of civil offices but under the offices of their particular banners.[28] But Han bannermen were ethnically Han and a part of

Han Chinese society as well. Consequently, they could function as intermediaries between the Han and the Manchus. This dual identity was sometimes useful for the Qing in controlling Han society. Han bannermen close to the Qing court often worked assiduously for the Manchus. The family history of Cao Xueqin (?–1763), the author of *Honglou meng* (*Dream of the Red Chamber*), provides a good illustration of the social situation of Han bannermen in the late seventeenth and early eighteenth centuries.

According to the account in *Qingshi gao* (Draft of the official Qing history), Cao's family had lived in Shenyang, in Fengtian Province, for generations.[29] Jonathan Spence has investigated in detail the history of the Cao family and the position of Han Chinese bondservants within the Eight Banner system. According to his study, when the Manchus conquered the Liaodong area in the 1620s, members of the Cao family surrendered to them and became attached to the Manchu Plain White Banner, as bondservants of the Neiwufu. They were later transferred to a Han Plain White Banner. Cao Xueqin's great grandfather, Cao Xi, was appointed president of the Board of Works (*gongbu shangshu*) during the reign of the Kangxi Emperor (1662–1722). Cao Xi's wife had been one of the Kangxi Emperor's nursemaids. Cao Xueqin's grandfather, Cao Yin (1658–1712), also a favorite of the Kangxi Emperor, was in 1690 appointed textile commissioner of the Neiwufu in Suzhou and later in Nanjing, where silk fabrics for the Qing court were woven. Cao Yin was also appointed salt censor of Lianghuai in 1704 and subsequently reappointed in 1706, 1708, and 1710. He was also a well-known literary man who patronized publication of such Chinese classics as the *Quan Tangshi* (The complete Tang poems).[30]

Cao Yin's real responsibility to the Manchu dynasty however, was to track the movements of officials and southern Chinese society in general. After the death of Cai Yin, Cao Fu (Cao Xueqin's father) succeeded him in this task. As private bureaucratic agents for the emperor, Cao Yin and Cao Fu compiled many private reports for the Kangxi Emperor based on the fruits of their investigations. Many of these accounts have been compiled in *Guanyu Jianing shizao Caojia dang'an shiliao* (Historical materials on the Cao family as textile factory head in Jianing). In them, Cao Yin and Cao Fu reported on such diverse matters as the price of rice, natural disasters, financial conditions, and the movement of merchants in the south.[31] Later, having incurred the Yongzheng Emperor's (1678–1735) wrath for neglect of his duties, Cao Fu was relieved of his post as textile commissioner, and the family's property was confiscated. It was after the ruin of his family that Cao Xueqin turned to the writing of *Honglou meng.* As a once privileged member of the Qing court, Cao Xueqin was well positioned to describe the lives of Manchu nobles in his novel.[32] The case of the Cao family clearly shows the high position that could be attained by Han bannermen during the Qing.[33]

The early Qing government also appointed many Han bannermen to important offices in its bureaucratic organization such as president (*shangshu*) of the Six Boards in Beijing and provincial governors-general. Han bannermen were expected to play a substantial role in pacifying Han society throughout China. Spence writes that in 1647 nine out of twelve officials with rank of governor-general were Han bannermen.[34]

The work of Narakino Shimesu examines the proportion of Manchu bannermen, Mongolian bannermen, Han bannermen, and civilian Han Chinese who attained high official positions during the Qing. According to Narakino, the percentage of Han bannermen among all governors-general between 1644 and 1670 was 77.7 percent (forty-nine out of sixty-three), while the percentage of Manchu bannermen and civilian Han Chinese was only 4.7 and 17.4 percent, respectively.[35]

Once the Qing established firm control over China, certainly by the eighteenth and nineteenth centuries, however, the bureaucratic opportunities for Han bannermen diminished. The proportion of Han bannermen who attained governor-generalship between 1881 and 1900 had dropped to only 1.8 percent (one out of fifty-three), while the proportions of Manchu bannermen and civilian Han Chinese who held this post were 26.4 and 67.9 percent, respectively.[36] After the pacification of China, Han Chinese who passed the civil service examinations began claiming posts in the Qing bureaucracy. Of their number only a few Han bannermen held important positions in the Qing administration, even though they, like the family of Cao Xueqin, still worked for the Qing court.

Confronted by intense anti-Qing movements at the beginning of the twentieth century, the Qing once again expected Han bannermen to play an important role as intermediaries between themselves and the majority Han. For a sense of modern Manchurian history it is worth examining the case of Zhao Erxun, Shengjing military governor from 1905 to 1907 and governor-general of the Three Eastern Provinces from 1911 to 1912. Zhao was a Han

Plain Blue Bannerman and a native of Manchuria's Fenghuang subprefecture (*ting*). Southern Manchuria had been governed by the Shengjing military governor since the beginning of the Qing; this position was held only by Manchu bannermen because the Qing considered Manchuria their homeland.[37] After the Russo-Japanese War, however, the Manchus realized that Han officials could govern the Han Chinese society of this area more effectively than Manchu bannermen.

Zhao Erxun is well known as the first Han to be appointed Shengjing military governor; the appointment occurred in 1905. He was able to hold this office, however, only because, as a Han bannerman, he was close to the ruling dynasty. In addition, according to the *Fengtian tongzhi* (Local gazetteer of Fengtian), Zhao's family had lived in Liaoyang for generations. His father, Zhao Wenying, and his brothers Zhao Erzhen and Zhao Ercui all held *jinshi* (metropolitan graduate) degrees.[38] Another brother, Zhao Erfeng, became the governor-general of Sichuan at the end of the Qing period and was killed in Sichuan during the 1911 Revolution.[39] Thus, we can see that Zhao Erxun came from an influential Fengtian family. The fact that he later became head compiler of the *Qingshi gao* further illustrates his intimate relationship with the Qing court.

As I will discuss in chapter 3, China's dynasties, including the Qing, prohibited high officials from holding office in their native provinces. In spite of this regulation (called *benji huibi* or "rule of avoidance"), Zhao Erxun became the Shengjing military governor and governor-general of the Three Eastern Provinces because of his bannerman status. Bannermen did not come under the jurisdiction of the rule of avoidance and the Han banners, rather than their native provinces, were considered their domiciles. Thus his dual identity as both Han *and* bannerman made Zhao Erxun's appointments possible.

Because Han bannermen were regarded as both bannermen and Han people, their social situation could be truly complicated. It is true that many Han, in their position under the banners' jurisdiction, enjoyed a privileged status even though they lacked full status as regular bannermen.[40] The pardon by the Qing dynasty of Zhang Rong, the son of a wealthy Han bannerman in Fushun County, is a good example. The story is related in the article "Xinhai geming yu Zhang Rong" (The 1911 Revolution and Zhang Rong), written by Qin Chengzhi. Zhang Rong, a Han Bordered Yellow Bannerman, was a Fengtian leader in the anti-Qing movement at the time of the 1911

Revolution. It is said that the Zhang family had originally immigrated from Jinan in Shandong Province at the beginning of the Qing period, and worked hereditarily as subordinates in the office of the Sanling. So their family members were Han bannermen in the sense that they were Han in the banner system. Beginning after the Russo-Japanese War, Zhang Rong became active in the anti-Qing movement, and with his friend Wu Yue, plotted to assassinate five Qing ministers in Beijing in 1905 as they set out on a tour of Western countries to observe constitutional governments. The assassination failed: Wu Yue was killed by his own bomb and Zhang Rong was arrested.

As an influential family of Han bannermen who had managed the Qing emperors' tombs in Fengtian since the beginning of the dynasty, the Zhang family maintained strong connections within the Qing court. Zhang Rong's elder sister, Zhang Gui, used the family's status to bribe a powerful eunuch, Li Lianying (?–1911) to advocate on her brother's behalf. According to the description in "Xinhai geming yu Zhang Rong," Li Lianying prevailed upon the Empress Dowager, saying, "Zhang Rong is like one of our sons because he belongs to our family [banners]. May I suggest that we spare him?" Zhang Rong escaped the death penalty and was instead jailed in Tianjin. Later, he escaped from jail and fled to Japan, only to return to Fengtian later to lead the revolutionary movement.[41]

At the same time, the Han bannermen's special relationship with the Qing court made their social situation difficult. In the Han community there was deep-seated hatred of Han bannermen, maybe especially those who served the Manchus during their conquest of China.[42] The Qing thus had to protect those Han who had been adopted into its banner system, a situation that seems to have lasted throughout the dynasty. "Jinggao Hanjun ji baoyi qiren wen" (Warning to Han bannermen and banner bondservants), written by an unnamed revolutionary, describes the circumstances in which Han bannermen found themselves on the eve of the 1911 Revolution.

> Han bannermen have been eager to acquire full status as bannermen during the past 260 years. Yet, the Manchus consider them outsiders, while the Han people shun them as bannermen [traitors]. There is no ethnic group (*minzu*) to which the Han bannermen belong, and no place for them to go.[43]

Mark Elliott discusses the problem of ethnic identity for the Manchus, but the Han bannermen also faced a serious problem: they could face rejection from both Han Chinese and Manchus. It is true that while some Han bannermen like Yuan Jinkai and Zhang Huanxiang (Zhang Rong's cousin, 1880–1962) tendered their loyalty to the Qing court, others like Zhang Rong harbored hostility toward it. Nonetheless, they shared similar circumstances in Chinese society.

As a result, some Han bannermen formed special ties and created their own networks. As mentioned earlier, about 17.8 percent of Fengtian's total registered population in 1908 was Han bannermen, and some of them exerted great influence over their local society. Amagai Kenzaburō has explained the bonds that developed from generation to generation between wealthy Han banner families in Fengtian. Once acquainted with one wealthy family of Han bannermen who were manorial managers, Amagai quickly gained access to other locally powerful Han bannermen.[44] This network played an important role in Fengtian politics at the time of the 1911 Revolution.

In addition to Zhao Erxun, Zhang Rong, and Yuan Jinkai, there were other prominent leaders among the Han bannermen in Fengtian at the time.[45] Wu Jinglian (1874–1944), a Han Plain Yellow Bannerman and native of Ningyuan County, was elected chairman of the Fengtian Provincial Assembly in 1909 and led the constitutional movement there. After the 1911 Revolution, he entered the world of national politics and was elected speaker of the House of Representatives.[46] Wang Yuquan, a Han Plain Blue Bannerman and native of Haichang County, was also elected to the Provincial Assembly and was sent to the National Assembly (*zizhengyuan*) as a Fengtian provincial delegate in 1909.[47]

Many Han bannermen in Fengtian were key figures in local politics where they formed a world of local elites. According to Yuan's diary, *Yonglu jingguo zishu*, Yuan Jinkai's daughter, Yuan Qingbin, married a cousin of Zhang Rong, Zhang Huanying. Even Yuan Jinkai and Zhang Rong, who were politically at opposite poles, maintained a close relationship.[48] Yuan Jinkai also had a strong connection to Zhao Erxun, and after the 1911 Revolution Yuan joined him as one of the compilers of the *Qingshi gao*.[49] Many other local leaders who may have belonged to the Han banners were not noted as such in local Fengtian gazetteers after the abolition of the civil service examinations, which had been an occasion for recording banner affiliations.[50]

Furthermore, former Han bannermen generally dared not reveal their identity in the fiercely anti-Manchu climate that accompanied the 1911 Revolution. Zhao Erxun obviously had full status as a Han bannerman (*zhengshen qiren*). Other than his case, however, it is now difficult to clarify just what status specific Han people had in the banner system late in the Qing period.

These powerful Han bannermen elites sometimes held large tracts of land in their home villages, and as landlords some of them exercised great influence over the local people and the land. How these men became major landowners has significant bearing upon modern Manchurian history, and an examination of these Han bannermen landlords can reveal the specific historical features of the Fengtian local elite.

CHAPTER 2

Fengtian's Land System at The End of the Qing

Han Bannermen Landlords

It is generally held that landlordism in Manchuria was less significantly developed than in other areas of China such as the lower Yangzi valley and southern China. A series of research reports on the condition of Manchurian villages conducted by the Manzhouguo government in the 1930s confirmed the tendency toward egalitarian land distribution in Manchu villages.[1] However, it is also true that there were powerful landlords in Manchuria in the first half of the twentieth century. According to Amano Motonosuke's investigation in 1928, influential officials in the Zhang Zuolin government, such as Zhang Zuolin himself, Gao Qinghe, Zeng Youyi (b. 1871?), and Zhang Huanxiang, all owned vast areas of land in Fengtian Province at that time (Table 2).[2] Even though landlordism is not necessarily a dominant feature of modern Manchurian history, it is important to recognize that leading figures in Fengtian political circles controlled large tracts of land. How did they acquire so much land? To answer this question, we need to consider the process by which banner and official lands in Fengtian were disposed of by the government there from the beginning of the twentieth century.

By the late 1920s, some of Fengtian's most powerful landlords were Han bannermen. According to Sonoda Kazuki, a well-informed Japanese journalist working in Fengtian during the first half of the twentieth century, Zhang Rong's family, which belonged to the Han Bordered Yellow Banner, was regarded as the area's wealthiest landlord family.[3] Their ancestors had emigrated from Jinan in Shandong Province at the beginning of the Qing, and lived in Fushun, about forty kilometers east of the city of Fengtian. There they served for

Table 2. Land Owned by Top Officials of the Zhang Zuolin Government, 1928

Name	Acreage	Estimated Value	Location
Zhang Zuolin	1,100 *shang*	Unknown	Beizhen
	500 *shang*	Unknown	Heishan
	150,000 *shang*	Unknown	Unknown
Zhang Huanxiang	200 *shang*	5,000 *yuan*	Huadian
(Governor, Special District of the Three Eastern Provinces)	1,200 *shang*	40,000 *yuan*	Fushun
Zhang Zuoxiang	600 *mu*	Unknown	Jin-xian
(Governor-general of the	300 *mu*	Unknown	Beizhen
Three Eastern Provinces)	100 *mu*	Unknown	Beizhen
Zeng Youyi (Director of the Dongqing Railroad)	300 *shang*	200,000 *yuan*	Shenyang
Gao Qinghe (Secretary General of Foreign Affairs)	Unknown	140,000 *yuan*	Jinxi
Wang Shuhan	100 *shang*	50,000 *yuan*	Shenyang
(Former Governor of Fengtian Province)	5,000 *fang*	150,000 *yuan*	Jilin province
Peng Xian	Unknown	350,000 *yuan*	Liaozhong
(Director General of the Bank of Dongsansheng)	Unknown	600,000 *yuan*	Liaoyang
Guan Dingbao (Secretary General of Internal Affairs)	Unknown	140,000 *yuan*	Liaoyang
Bao Kang (Director General of Military Provisions)	Unknown	300,000 *yuan*	Shenyang
Qi Enming (Director General of Matters of Public Order)	80 *shang*	60,000 *yuan*	Zhangwu
Yang Yuting (Advisory Councilor)	350 *shang*	20,000 *yuan*	Faku
Liu Shanqing	Unknown	420,000 *yuan*	Tieling
(Acting Governor of Fengtian Province)	Unknown	220,000 yuan	Kushan

Source: Amano Motonosuke, *Manshū keizai no hattatsu* (Minami Manshū Tetsudō Kabushiki Kaisha, 1932), 39–41.

generations in the Office of the Sanling, which was responsible for the Qing ancestral graves, and in this capacity they managed the Sanling itself and the extensive lands belonging to it. The tomb of Nurhaci (Fuling or Dongling) and that of Hong Taiji (Zhaoling or Beiling) were located in the eastern suburb and the northern outskirts of the city of Fengtian, respectively, while the tomb of their ancestors (Yongling) lay in the western part of Xinbin County, about one hundred and twenty kilometers east of the city of Fengtian. A vast area of land belonging to the Sanling lay in the central and eastern parts of Fengtian Province and the southern part of Jilin Province.

At the end of the Qing period, Zhang Qinshan, Zhang Rong's father, was said to own about 19,200 *mu* (six *mu* were approximately equal to one acre) of land in Xifeng County and about 10,000 *mu* of land around the city of Fengtian. As the owner of two grain warehouses (*liangchan*) in Fushun and Xingjing counties and a brewery (*shaoguo*) in Tonghua County, he also engaged in commerce and manufacturing there.[4] It is not certain whether Zhang Qinshan officially owned the land in the Qing period, but there is no doubt that he controlled large holdings in Xifeng County and the city of Fengtian. Other members of the Zhang family also became well-known landlords after the 1911 Revolution. Zhang Huanxiang, Zhang Rong's cousin, owned more than 5,600 *mu* of land in Xian County in 1928;[5] he was a high-ranking official in both the Zhang Zuolin and Manzhouguo regimes. Another relative, Zhang Huanyu, was also a powerful landlord in Fushun and was elected a member of the Provincial Assembly in 1909.[6]

In contrast to Zhang Rong, who was a leader of the anti-Qing movement in Fengtian, Yuan Jinkai was a leader of the Qing loyalists in Fengtian at the time of the 1911 Revolution. He was not a major landlord, but he possessed more than 500 *mu* of land in his home village, Shanyaopu, in Liaoyang. Yuan's ancestor, Yuan Bingyi, had surrendered to the Manchu army before the Qing entered China proper. His family belonged to the Han Plain Yellow Banner and family members held hereditary positions as subordinates of the Board of Rites in Shengjing.[7]

Many other Han bannerman landlords were based in Fengtian, such as Wang Chengxian, a member of the Han Bordered Blue Banner who owned at least 7,500 *mu* of land in the Liaoyang area. His family hereditarily held the position of manager on a Qing noble's manor.[8] Some of the powerful landlords in Fengtian had been managers of the Neiwufu manors, including

Tian Yugong and Ling Yunge. As in the case of Ling Yunge, Tian's family belonged to the Han Plain Yellow Banner and its eldest son inherited the position of *zhuangtou* to the Neiwufu manors in Liaoyang.[9] Amagai Kenzaburō explains that Han bannermen, especially *zhuangtou* of the former manors, were sometimes very wealthy, controlling land and peasants in their rural communities. According to his report, the word *zhuangtou* itself was used to designate the influential men of the local villages.[10]

Clearly, by the end of the Qing, some Han bannermen had emerged as landlords and local elites in Fengtian. To understand how this came about, we must first examine Fengtian's land system during the Qing period.

The Basic Structure of the Qing Land System

The Qing government officially established Fengtian Province in 1907. The registered population of the Fengtian area (the term "Fengtian Province" was used only after 1907) was only 359,622 in 1741; however, it reached 10,238,309 by 1908, an increase of approximately 28.4 times (Table 3). During the Qing period many peasants migrated from provinces in China proper, such as Shandong and Henan, to Manchuria and settled there, cultivating extensive areas of land. As a result, the amount of land under cultivation in Manchuria rapidly increased. The registered cultivated land in Fengtian reached 41,695,340 *mu* in 1908, while it had been only 2,524,321 *mu* in 1753, an increase of about 16.5 times over 150 years (Table 4). Although the official data did not indicate actual acreage, these figures are evidence of the clear trend that cultivated land in Fengtian Province was rapidly increasing. While demographic analysis of Fengtian society in the Qing period is certainly of great importance to the study of Manchurian history, the focus here will be Fengtian's Qing period land system under which these increases in population and cultivated land were realized.

Although the Qing land system in Fengtian was extremely complicated, we can summarize its basic structure. According to Sudō Yoshiyuki's study, the total land, including wasteland, was divided into the "civil area" (*minjie*) and the "banner area" (*qijie*). Land in the civil area was regarded as "civil land" and was placed under the control of such civilian offices as county magistrates. Han civilians (*minren*) were permitted to own only civil land.

Land in the banner area was considered "banner land" in a broad sense, or "official land," and it was placed under the control of the banner offices. Official land consisted of the banner land for bannermen, various types of manors owned by the Qing court and its nobles, the Sanling's land, pastures controlled by Mongol nobles, wasteland, and so forth.[11] In short, only the Qing court, its nobles, and its bannermen were allowed to own official lands. The greater part of the land in Fengtian was classified as official and banner land. As Table 4 shows, 21,997,681 *mu* out of a total of 28,495,912 *mu* in Fengtian (77.1 percent) was regarded as official and banner land in 1887. As mentioned earlier, compared to the scarce information we have about manors owned by Qing nobles and the lands possessed by the bannermen, our knowledge about the official manor system is better developed. My explanation of the land system in Manchuria, therefore, will center on the Qing official manors.

Table 3. Registered Civil Population of Fengtian Province, 1741–1931

Year	Population
1741	359,622[a]
1781	789,093[a]
1851	2,582,000[b]
1861	2,827,000[b]
1871	2,969,000[b]
1881	4,208,000[b]
1891	4,617,000[b]
1908	10,238,309[c]
1931	16,366,175[d]

Sources: a) *Shengjing tongzhi* (Qianlong 48 edition), *juan* 35, "Hukou"; b) Li Wenzhi, ed. *Zhongguo jindai nongyeshi ziliao* (Collected sources of agricultural history in modern China)(Beijing: Sanlian shudian, 1957), vol. 1, 10–15; c) *Manshū chihō-shi*, vol. 1, (Kantō Totoku-fu, 1911), 12; d) *Dongbei nianjian* (Minguo 20 edition; Dongbei Wenhuashe, 1932), 150.

The lands of the official manors, such as those of the Neiwufu, occupied about 10 percent of the official and banner lands in Fengtian in 1887 (2,233,198 *mu* out of the total registered acreage of 21,997,681 *mu*) (Table 5). The vast holdings owned by Qing nobles were also classified as banner lands. The *zhuangtou*, or managers, controlled these lands, and their subordinates (*zhuangding*) cultivated them. All were Han bannermen. As the recent studies mentioned in chapter 1 have shown, a considerable number of the immigrants from China proper also came to be organized under the banner system and engaged in the cultivation of manor lands and banner lands.

Table 4. Acreage of Registered Cultivated Land in Fengtian Province, 1661–1931

Year	Acreage (*mu*)
1661	60,933[a]
1685	311,750[a]
1724	580,658[a]
1753	2,524,321[a]
1851	11,524,171[a]
1887	28,495,912[a]
Total Official Land	21,997,681
Total Civil Land	6,498,231
1908	41,695,340[b]
1931	93,144,260[c]
Total Official Land	1,018,675
Total Civil Land	92,125,585

Sources: a) Liang Fangzhong, *Zhongguo lidai hukou tiandi tianfu tongji* (Shanghai renmin chubanshe, 1980), 380, 384–85; b) *Manshū chihō-shi*, vol. 1 (Kantō Totoku-fu, 1911), 140; c) *Dongbei nianjian* (Minguo 20 edition) (Dongbei wenhuashe, 1932), 112.

It was also true that these *zhuangtou* and *zhuangding* often sublet manor lands to Han civil peasants who had emigrated from China proper later than the *zhuangtou* and *zhuangding*, and who were not enrolled in the banner system. A large portion of the manor lands was actually cultivated by these Han immigrants and their descendants over the latter half of the Qing period.

In addition, some of the land that had been newly settled by Han peasants was placed under the control of the manor offices because these lands were supposed to lie within the banner area. Once the *zhuangtou* and their subordinates became aware of the newly cultivated lands, they required the Han settlers to pay rents to the manor offices. They insisted that the newly cultivated lands within the banner area were the holdings of manors.

The Han peasants could do nothing about this and were obliged to obey. Since most of the wasteland in Fengtian Province was originally considered to lie within the banner area, the acreage of official lands rapidly expanded along with the increase in land settlement.

Table 5. Registered Acreage of Official Land in Fengtian in 1887, by Type (*mu*)*

Bannerland, including manors owned by Manchu nobles	14,349,959
Newly settled bannerland	1,432,140
Bannerland permanently rented by civilians	287,669
Manors owned by the Neiwufu	1,941,542
Other official manors	265,124
Pastureland	1,294,674
Former hunting grounds	120,900
Newly settled wasteland in eastern frontier	2,278,000
Gardens of the court	26,532
Land for tombs	141
Total	21,997,681

Source: Liang Fangzhong, *Zhongguo lidai hukou tiandi tianfu tongji* (Shanghai renmin chubanshe, 1980), 385.

* Sanling land is not included in this table.

The *zhuangtou* of the manors collected rents (*zu*) from their *zhuangding* and tenant peasants. They in turn paid annual rents to the manor owners, such as Qing nobles, the Neiwufu office, and so forth. For example, the annual rents for the Neiwufu office, called Neiwufu *zu,* were not only paid in cash, but also in kind, as explained in the first chapter. We do not have an exact figure for the amount of the annual rents. But concerning rent payments in cash, we do know that in the later Qing period, each *zhuangtou* of the Neiwufu manors in Suizhong County was supposed to pay from 119 to 145 *liang* (an "ounce" of silver or a tael) per year. And at the close of the Qing period, these *zhuangtou* collected from 1 to 4.5 *yuan* per *mu* in rent from their *zhuangding* and tenant peasants.[12] According to *Kōsan* by Amagai Kenzaburō, at the end of the Qing period one *yuan* was equal to between 0.5 and 0.6 *liang.*[13] If a *zhuangtou* leased 3,000 *mu* of manor land to tenants at the rate of 2 *yuan* per *mu* of rent, he could collect about 3,000 to 3,600 *liang* from them. Although a certain amount of cash was needed by the *zhuangtou* to run the manor, rents squeezed from his subordinates still served as a source of profit for the manor manager.

This situation changed after the Russo-Japanese War. At that time a great deal of land not originally controlled by either the civil or banner offices still remained unregistered and untaxed. But at the end of the Qing period, and then again after the 1911 Revolution, the acreage of registered, taxed land increased enormously. Even though a considerable area of uncultivated land was actually settled by peasant immigrants from China proper in this period, the rapid increase in the registered acreage of cultivated land was mainly a product of an improved record-keeping system. That is, a new land survey carried out by the Fengtian provincial government after the Russo-Japanese War was able to identify and record the extent and location of heretofore unregistered land.

The reorganization of the land system at the end of the Qing period was responsible for the transformation of official land into civil land. And after the 1911 Revolution, the disposition of official land to private civilians continued to be carried out by local governments under the Republic and the Zhang Zuolin regime. The Tunkenju (Bureau of Land Settlement) and the Guandi qingzhangju (Bureau for the Disposition of Official Land) were established in 1913 and 1915 for this purpose. A report by the Land Bureau of Manzhouguo explains the actual process of the disposition of official land conducted in Fengtian Province after the 1911 Revolution. As Table 6 shows, 11,775,000 *mu* of the former official land in Fengtian were sold to private individuals from 1913 through 1924. Former manors owned by the Qing offices and its nobles were completely disposed of through this undertaking.[14] Consequently, by 1931 official land in Fengtian occupied only 1,018,675 *mu* out of 93,144,260 *mu* (only about 1 percent) of the total registered land (see Table 4). The point here is, a considerable portion of formerly official land, reorganized into civil land, fell into the hands of former Han bannermen, the very people who had earlier managed and cultivated it as official land. This process effectively privatized official lands in Fengtian. This raises the question of how the Han bannermen managed to assume ownership of lands that had formerly been retained by the Qing court and its nobles. Through this inquiry, we may learn how those bannermen came to be powerful landlords in Fengtian at the end of the Qing period and after the 1911 Revolution.

Table 6. Acreage of Official Land Disposed of after the 1911 Revolution in Fengtian (*mu*)

1) Acreage of official lands disposed of by the Guandi Qingzhangju, 1915–1930	10,081,920
Classification:	
Public manors owned by the Neiwufu	654,101
Manors owned by Manchu nobles	2,093,309
Wasteland	2,937,413
Newly settled land	48,838
Land of the Sanling	1,101,753
Mountainous land	2,431,676
Public land permanently rented by civilians	67,142
Former pastureland	540,033
2) Acreage of official land managed by the Eight Banner soldiers and disposed of by the Tunkenju, 1913–1924	1,693,241

Source: Manshū ni okeru tochi seido no gaiyō (Manshūkoku Tochikyoku, 1935), 42–53.

Han Bannermen as Pseudo-Landlords

As we have seen, when the Qing conquered Liaodong at the beginning of the seventeenth century, many Han landowners offered their allegiance and their lands to the Qing in return for protection. Much of this land was then owned by the Qing court and its nobles and organized as various kinds of official and banner land as well as individual noble estates. The former landowners became bannermen and, in the case of the noble estates, some were appointed *zhuangtou* of the manors. Peasants who had cultivated these lands under the original landlords were usually included in the system as banner people and tilled the land as before, but now under the oversight of the *zhuangtou.*[15]

There were two reasons why the Qing appointed many of the former landlords as *zhuangtou* of the manors. First, as landlords these Han had been influential people in their villages, and therefore, the dynasty could rule the lands and the cultivators more effectively through the former power-holders. Second, since Han people were generally good farmers, it was believed the Qing could better harness their agricultural skills by retaining the former Han landlords as managers. The *zhuangtou* post was hereditary, and its duties were to manage land and peasants and pay annual rent to the Qing court and its nobles.[16] The Qing tried to insure Manchu financial dominance by establishing the manors as their private economic base.

Although their various holdings, including their manors and the annual rents received from them, supported the Qing court and its nobles, they were unable to participate in the actual running of the manors. Control had to be placed in the hands of the *zhuangtou*, and this led to serious problems in the Manchurian manor system: On one hand, the Qing depended upon these properties and had to protect the authority its agents, the *zhuangtou*, exercised over the land and peasants. On the other hand, the court and its nobles had to check the growth of *zhuangtou* power because it had the potential to challenge their effective ownership of the land. Only absolute power as conquerors guaranteed the Manchus' status as owners. If their power weakened, the position of both the court and its nobles on the manor lands could become precarious.

In fact, the problems that resulted from the court and nobles loosening their control over the manors were recognized relatively early in the Qing period. A report by Sun Jiagan (1683–1753), a government official of the mid-Qing, reveals much general information about the manors in Fengtian and describes the situation as follows:[17]

> Recently the bannermen [the Qing nobles] have been suing their tenant peasants for not paying annual rents and trying to confiscate the land from them. For their part, the tenant peasants lodge objections against the bannermen's claims. As a matter of fact, all of these problems are caused by subordinates of the bannermen, such as their slaves who are sent to the banner lands [the manors] in Manchuria to collect annual rents, the *zhuangtou* of the banner lands who collect annual rents from the tenant peasants, and the agents of the *zhuangtou*. If the peasants want to get good farmlands, they have to work hard to settle, fertilize, and cultivate those lands for two or three years. However, after they have finished cultivating the lands, the subordinates of the bannermen sue them for occupying land belonging to the banners. In this way, the banner lands expand and the *zhuangtou* can collect more rent, but they do not pass on these increases to the bannermen. The bannermen are robbed of their lands, and the tenant peasants subjected to forced collection of annual rents by the *zhuangtou*. The *zhuangtou* and their subordinates embezzle the annual rents and share them. Then they collect the following year's rents from the tenant peasants

> to pay the bannermen. Then in the following year the *zhuangtou* are not able to collect rents. So the *zhuangtou*, being afraid of reproach by the bannermen, report that the peasants will not pay the annual rent. So, the bannermen sue their tenants, and the tenants lodge a protest against the bannermen. So on the one hand, the bannermen are suffering from the lack of annual rents though they own the lands. On the other hand, the tenant peasants are threatened with the confiscation of lands they have cultivated even though they pay their rents regularly. Only the *zhuangtou* and their subordinates [win], living a luxurious life by embezzling rents from the banner lands.[18]

Sun Jiagan unequivocally blames the *zhuangtou* and their subordinates for embezzling annual rents. Because of this malfeasance, Qing nobles were not able to collect sufficient revenue. The *zhuangtou* had allowed the Han Chinese peasants to settle on uncultivated lands, which were then absorbed into the manor properties. This made the Han peasants their tenants, and these peasants were then faced with the forced collection of rents by the *zhuangtou*. Through this process, the *zhuangtou* extended the lands under their management. Some *zhuangtou* accumulated great wealth by exploiting the peasants, while the real owners of the manors faced increasing financial difficulties. Sun's account of the *zhuangtou*'s local power might be somewhat exaggerated, but he gives voice to a deep-seated complaint the court and nobles had with the management of their manors. This is the more striking because Sun himself was not a Manchu noble.

The concentration of actual power over the manors in the hands of the *zhuangtou* continued until the later Qing. The following report by Zhang Tingxiang, another government official, describes the situation in the Daoguang period (1821–1850).[19] It is typical of such reports in that it, too, is critical of *zhuangtou* misconduct:

> The *zhuangtou* of the Jinzhou manor, Gao Lin, enjoyed considerable local power. His name was well known even in the imperial court. He always blew his own horn and kept many concubines. He treated the peasants harshly. Indeed, his unlawful deeds were innumerable.[20]

This document suggests that the Neiwufu manors in Jinzhou did not necessarily provide economic support for the Qing court alone. As Amagai reports, some *zhuangtou* became very wealthy through their managerial powers and wielded considerable influence in the villages of southern Manchuria.[21] Given the persistence of these tendencies, the Qing court found itself inclined to reorganize the manorial and official land systems in Fengtian Province after the Russo-Japanese War.

The Disposition of Official Lands

Confronted by the crises of the Russian and Japanese invasions, the Qing government tried to reorganize its control over Manchuria. The basic administrative structure was changed from a military to a civil system in 1907, which meant that Manchuria was placed under the same administrative system as other provinces.[22] One of the key reform programs in Fengtian was the transformation of official land into civil land. Underlying this was the Qing dynasty's realization that official land no longer functioned as a private economic resource for the Manchus, especially since the proceeds from manors increasingly fell into the hands of the *zhuangtou*. A large portion of the official lands was already controlled by these pseudo-landlords, the Han bannermen, on whom the dynasty had bestowed the right to manage its manors.

The Qing government undertook the disposition of official lands in Fengtian in 1901. At the close of the Russo-Japanese War, the Fengtian provincial government under the Qing conducted a full-scale land survey and sold a vast area of official lands to private civilians. As we will detail later, certain Han bannermen such as the manor *zhuangtou* became eligible as private civilians to purchase official lands they had formerly managed. The privatization project was extended by the Fengtian provincial government under the Republic, and later by the Zhang Zuolin government. Thus, disposition of official lands, including the manors, continued from the end of the Qing into the Republican period.[23]

The purpose of this project was twofold. First of all, the government wanted to certify ownership of specific land parcels: title-recipients would pay for the land and be responsible for paying taxes on it. This was essentially a cadastral survey through which the Fengtian provincial government wished to establish ownership and tax responsibilities. Moreover, through this project the government sought to increase its economic and political control over local landlords and, through them, the villages.

The second purpose was to generate immediate revenue. The Qing government needed an enormous amount of money to implement the various reform programs in Fengtian. According to the calculations of the second governor-general, Xiliang, in 1910 the Fengtian provincial government annually needed 2.5 million *liang* to re-establish a police system, 2 million *liang* to establish a new judicial system, and 4.4 million *liang* to the reorganize the educational system.[24] Xiliang also explained that the annual revenue of the Fengtian provincial government was only 15.8 million *liang* in 1908.[25] Facing financial crisis, the Qing bureaucrats of Fengtian Province became highly interested in selling official land, from which they could also expect regular revenue in the future through taxes.

The important point here is that Han bannermen, especially certain of the *zhuangtou* on the manors, were perfectly positioned to buy the land they had been managing. By purchasing or simply occupying these lands, Han bannermen who had been pseudo-landlords began to acquire the status of true landlords.

To illustrate how the government disposed of official land, data from the *Dongsansheng zhenglüe* on Fengtian has been tabulated (Table 7).[26] First the provincial government identified sixteen specific areas regarded as official land under the traditional Qing land system. All land within these areas was designated as available for sale to private citizens. We can classify these areas into three groups. The first consisted of uncultivated lands, which had been reserved for Manchu bannermen (areas 1, 2, 4, and 7–11). The second consisted of lands part of the official manors, such as the Neiwufu manors (areas 3, 5, and 6). The third involved pastureland originally held by Mongol bannermen (areas 12–16). A large portion of these lands was already under cultivation by Han Chinese peasants.

The provincial government established an office in the nearest district capital of each area that was subject to the disposition. The office, called Kenwuju (Office of Land Settlement), dispatched officials who surveyed the land, examined the landholding structure, and decided on the ownership of a particular parcel. Then the provincial government issued a deed to the certified landowner, who paid for the land and assumed responsibility for paying the land tax.

Table 7. Disposition of Official Land in Fengtian Province at the End of the Qing

A Areas Disposed	B Year of Disposal	C Acreage Disposed	D Total Revenue (*liang*)	E Revenue, 1907-1908 (*liang*)	F Land Price	G Land Tax
1. Qianfang dongliu weihuang	1901–1905	1,167,270 *mu*	1,451,029	None	1 *liang* 2 *qian* per *mu*	2 *fen* per *mu*
2. Qianfang xilu weihuang	1903–1905	3,031,788 *mu*	1,186,798	None		
3. Dalinghe muchang	1901–1902	509,190 *mu*	583,354	None	1st class: 2 *liang* 1 *qian* 2nd class: 1 *liang* 4 *qian* 3rd class: 7 *qian*	1–4 *fen*
4. Pansheyi kenwu	1903–1907	574,211 *mu*	321,089	None		1–3 *fen*
5. Jinshu guigongdi	1905–1907	213,770 *mu*	328,291	181,683		2–4 *fem*
6. Jinzhou guanzhuang	1906–	1,041,560 *mu*	1,809,729	941,589		6–8 *fen*
7. Niuzhuang weitang	1906–1908	385,522 *mu*	207,232	108,295		6–8 *fen*
8. Zhangwu qingzhang	1906–	2,637,499 *mu*	170,000	43,062	6 *qian* 6 *fen*	2 *fen*
9. Fengxiu shanhuang	1907–	1,232,750 *mu*	Not decided	10,259*	6 *qian*	2–5 *fen*
10. Fengxiu weitang	1907–	Not decided	Not decided	None	Same as (3) to (7)	2 *fen*
11. Dongliu fuzhang	1907–	Not decided	Not decided	150,000*		
12. Qianfang zasa ketu wangqi	1902–1904	625,000 *shang* 1,250,000 *zhang*	806,000	Not received	1st class: 4 *liang* 4 *qian* per *shang* 2nd class: 2 *liang* 4 *qian* 3rd class: 1 *liang* 4 *qian*	660 *wen* per *shang*
13. Xufang zasa ketu wangqi	1906–1907	89,063 *shang* 140,640 *zhang*	189,204	40,531		
14. Keerqin zhanguo gongqi	1904–1906	400,000 *shang*	327,037	None		
15. Tushen yetu	1906–	13,121 *fang*	Not decided	202,250		
16. Xufang zasa ketu zhenguo gongqi hebei meng huang	1908–	200,000 *shang*	Not decided	9,565**		

Source: *Dongsansheng zhenglüe*, *juan* 7, 3a–5b. Reprint, vol. 9, 5021–26 (Taipei: Chengwen chubanshe, 1965).

Notes: * Shengping silver

** Shiping silver

The disposition of Fengtian official lands was carried out from 1901 onwards for areas 1 and 3. The provincial government enlarged the projects under the direction of the *kenwu dachen* (minister of land settlements), Ting Jie, beginning in 1905.[27]

Land Price and Tax

Column (F) of Table 7 shows the price of land sold in these areas. Each area had its own regulated land price. However, seven out of sixteen of the areas had the same fixed price for cultivated land (areas 3–6, 8, 10, and 11). The best-quality land sold for 2 *liang* 1 *qian* per *mu*, the second-best for 1 *liang* 4 *qian*, and the third-best for 7 *qian*. Uncultivated land in those areas was sold at considerably lower prices.

The land in areas 1, 2, 7, and 9 was sold at lower prices due to its low productivity and disadvantageous location. Land that was originally pasture sold at the same fixed price. The best-quality land was sold at 4 *liang* 4 *qian* per *shang* (about 10 *mu*), the second-best at 3 *liang* 4 *qian*, and the third-best at 2 *liang* 4 *qian*. The provincial government also collected miscellaneous fees at the time of the sale of the official land.

Were these land prices reasonable compared to the average price of land at this time? We cannot give a definitive answer, but we do have a telling example: according to research conducted by the Fengtian Research Institute of Agriculture (Fengtian nongshi shiyanchang) in 1909, the average land price in Jinzhou Prefecture was about 8 *liang* per *mu*.[28] If this were the case, the Neiwufu's lands in Jinzhou (the Jinzhou manors) were disposed of at a price only about 20 percent of their average market value. Based on the data from the Jinzhou manors, it is highly likely that the provincial government set prices at a level considerably below market, because the land was sold to those who had strong customary rights to it.

Column (G) shows the land tax. The provincial government set the rate of the land tax at between 1 *fen* and 8 *fen* per *mu* in areas 1 through 11, based on the quality and location of the land. For example, because of its fertility and good location, land in the former Jinzhou manors was taxed at a higher rate than other land. The Jinzhou region had been a well-developed agricultural area since the early Qing, and a much of the land there had already been under cultivation even before the establishment of the manors in 1669.[29] Furthermore, at the close of the Qing period, the Jinzhou area also had good access to the railroad that connected northern China and Fengtian.

Acreage of Land Disposed

Column (C) indicates the amount of land sold in these areas. According to the figures, close to 7 million *mu* of land was sold by 1908, not counting the sale of former pasturelands. The provincial government continued to sell former official land thereafter. The total amount of registered land in Fengtian was about 40 million *mu* in 1908. The above figures show how widespread disposition of official land was at the end of the Qing. If we assume that the average plot cultivated by one Fengtian household was about 20 to 30 *mu*, 7 million *mu* equals enough land for 230,000 to 350,000 households.[30]

The Provincial Government's Revenue from Disposition of Official Lands

Columns (D) and (E) show provincial government revenue from this project. According to Column (D), the provincial government had already received about 4 million *liang* by 1908 through sales of official land in areas 1 through 5 and 8. Another 1.8 million *liang* was expected through the disposition of the Jinzhou manors (area 6). Xiliang's report later confirmed that the provincial government actually received more than 1.48 million *liang* by 1909 through the disposition of the Jinzhou manors.[31] Column (E) indicates that total revenue from the disposition of official land in 1907 and 1908 was about 1.64 million *liang*. According to Xiliang's report, the revenue of Fengtian Province in 1908 was about 15.8 million *liang*.[32] These figures show how important this income was to provincial government finances. It is highly likely that these revenues ensured sufficient funds for implementation of the reform programs in Fengtian.

Land Ownership by the Former Pseudo-Landlords

The next important question is, who had the right to purchase former official lands, both manor and banner lands? The basic principle the Qing government used here was to reorganize the official lands into civil lands without destroying the order of their rural communities and their existing social hierarchy. This meant that people who had actually controlled official lands in villages were granted first priority in the purchase of the land. A good illustration of this policy is the case of the Neiwufu manors.

According to the *Zhengzhi guanbao* (Official gazette) and the *Dongsansheng zhenglüe*, *zhuangtou* were granted a first option to purchase the Neiwufu manor lands they had previously managed. If the *zhuangtou* could not afford the purchase price for a particular piece of land, then the right of purchase passed to tenants of the manor. If neither the *zhuangtou* nor the tenants intended to purchase the land, the provincial government would sell it on the open market.[33]

The *zhuangtou* were granted these purchase opportunities for reasons rooted in both history and expedience. First of all, in some cases the ancestors of the *zhuangtou* had been landowners in this area during the Ming period and had commended themselves and their lands to the Manchu dynasty at the time of the Qing conquest. Therefore, by historical right, some of the *zhuangtou* had a special proprietary relationship to the land. Second, and more important, because the many *zhuangtou* of the manors who actually controlled the land and peasants during the Qing period were already functioning as landlords, they had come to form a local ruling class. As Amagai Kenzaburō reports, the Neiwufu manor *zhuangtou* were generally wealthy and thus the most able to meet the purchase price and taxes.[34]

Unfortunately, no document that systematically records the names of those who acquired ownership of the former Neiwufu manor lands has surfaced. We do, however, have fragmentary records concerning the disposition of the Neiwufu manors located in Jinzhou. The Jinzhou manors had been controlled by 216 *zhuangtou*, each of whom was supposed to manage 3,900–5,400 *mu* of land.[35] As Table 7 indicates, about 1.04 million *mu* of the Jinzhou manor lands were sold from 1906 to 1909.

The *zhuangtou* had to calculate the pros and cons of purchasing manor lands. To their advantage, they would acquire official ownership of the land. A disadvantage would be having to pay for the land and making subsequent tax payments. Xiliang wrote in his memoir that some of the *zhuangtou* schemed to obstruct the disposition of the Jinzhou manors because they did not want to pay the purchase price or tax on land they already controlled. According to Xiliang's report, other *zhuangtou*, on the contrary, were eager to purchase the lands they had managed, and many of them had the economic, political, and social power to do so. They welcomed the disposition of the Jinzhou manors because this would give them juridical ownership of the land. Finally there were also *zhuangtou* who could not afford to buy the manor lands and who, therefore, resisted their disposition.[36] Naturally, they feared of losing their rights to the land. Some of these *zhuangtou* borrowed money from merchants and then sold a part of the land to them to settle the debt.[37]

Confronted by the fact that the *zhuangtou* were granted first priority in acquiring landlord status, it was the tenants of the manors who had the strongest reservations about this project. They too feared losing their hereditary and customary rights to the land. On some manors, tenants whose families had cultivated the land since the manor's establishment or who had first brought the land under cultivation themselves were permitted to work the land indefinitely, so long as they paid rent. Under this arrangement, the *zhuangtou* were not able to raise the rent at will. This type of tenancy, called "permanent tenancy" (*yongdian quan*), was common in Fengtian.[38] But once the *zhuangtou* acquired full ownership of the land, those tenants' rights could be compromised or done away with. In response to the tenants' deep misgivings, the Qing government issued deeds confirming permanent tenancy on the land they had been cultivating, even after sale of that land to the *zhuangtou.* In addition, some wealthy tenants were also allowed to purchase parcels of the manor lands.[39]

According to Xu Shichang's memoir, a *zhuangtou* of one Jinzhou manor named Xu Chungsheng, a Han Plain Yellow bannerman, had previously controlled about 3,000 *mu*. When the Jinzhou manors were disposed of, both Xu and the manor's tenants had insisted on their right of purchase. In the end, Xu's family purchased more than 1,100 *mu* of land, while the 153 tenants managed to buy in total just over 1,800 *mu*.[40]

We have even more detailed information about how the right to purchase was pressed. An investigation conducted by the Land Bureau of the Manzhouguo government (Manshūkoku tochikyoku) in 1937 gives us a close look at how contested sales of manor land were sorted out.[41] Amagai Kenzaburō, a member of the research staff of the Land Bureau at that time, compiled a report on a continuing dispute over ownership of Jinzhou manor lands between a former manager and local peasants. To this end he conducted interviews and consulted their documents.

According to Amagai's report, the former *zhuangtou*, named Ling Yunge, a Han Plain Yellow Bannerman, had controlled more than 9,000 *mu* of manor land in Suizhong County in the Qing period. Back in the Ming period, Ling's family had lived in Dengzhou, Shandong Province. During the Ming-Qing transition, Ling Yunge's ancestor, Ling Sancai, had been an official under the Ming general Kong Youde, and in 1669 he was appointed *zhuangtou* of a manor in the Suizhong area as a reward for his meritorious deeds during the Qing conquest. It is said that twenty-five Han officers were appointed manor managers for the Neiwufu in Jinzhou at that time. Many of them, like Lin, were originally from Dengzhou in Shandong. Now they belonged to the banners and functioned as subordinates of the Neiwufu.

Subsequently, the eldest sons of the Ling family held the post of *zhuangtou* by inheritance. During the Jiaqing period (1796–1820), the Ling family controlled lands and peasants in the village of Lingjia and its neighborhood, overseeing about 3,600 *mu* of land in Lingjia and 5,400 *mu* in its western suburbs. The lands in Lingjia were original manor lands. The Ling family extended those manor lands toward western areas of Suizhong County, called *qianwei beidi* (northern areas of the front military station), over the later Qing period.

At the time of the disposition of the Jinzhou manors, Ling Yunge, the twelfth direct descendant of Ling Sancai, insisted that his family had the right to buy manor lands in accordance with the Qing regulations. But fifty-three tenants of the manor also pressed their own rights to purchase the same land. They explained that their ancestors immigrated into this area from Laizhou and Dengzhou in 1663 and that they had settled on and cultivated the land even before the establishment of the manors. Indeed, the Neiwufu had granted them the right of permanent tenancy. After negotiations between Ling Yunge and the tenants, the latter were permitted to buy a mere fraction, only about 640 *mu* of land, while Ling's family was allowed to purchase the rest. However, the peasants were still granted permanent tenancy on the land that Ling now owned. After the 1911 Revolution, Ling appealed to the government to deny the peasants their permanent tenancy, while the peasants continued the campaign to maintain their rights. As of the Manzhouguo period, the dispute remained unsettled.

These cases strongly suggest that powerful *zhuangtou* of the Jinzhou manors, Han Plain Yellow bannermen in particular, were able to muscle their way to purchasing a large portion of the former manor lands in a process that seems to have met the expectations of Qing officials.

From Pseudo-Landlords to Landlords: The Case of the Zhang Family

In addition to the *zhuangtou*, other Han bannermen were also given the opportunity to purchase or simply occupy considerable portions of the lands they had previously managed. The Zhang family, mentioned above, is a case in point.

The Zhang family controlled vast land holdings in the Fushun, Xian, Tonghua, and Xifeng areas at the end of the Qing period.[42] A large section of this land had originally been appended to the Sanling properties. As part of the official orthodoxies of the time, it was believed that a long stretch of *longmo* (the dragon stream) extended from Changbai Mountain through Zhaoling (the tomb of Hong Taiji) in Fengtian, and that this was a channel of the special energy, *longqi* (dragon spirit), which sustained the Qing dynasty. Changbai Mountain was the Manchu people's spiritual homeland, where they believed their first ancestor had been born in ancient times. The Qing dynasty cherished the *longmo* and set up the Sanling office to oversee the areas through which it passed.[43] It is highly likely that, from the end of the Qing period and after the 1911 Revolution, the Zhang family had successfully established their ownership of certain consecrated lands originally controlled by the Sanling office. The following case strongly supports this hypothesis.

A document (No. 32765) of the Office of Fengtian Province (Fengtian sheng gongshu), now deposited in the Archival Museum of Liaoning Province (Liaoning sheng dang'anguan), deals with incidents concerning Sanling land. One incident involved the attempted sale of part of a special zone within the old Sanling holdings. The zone, covering about 30,000 *mu*, was known as Zhaoling yaochai guandiandi (Official land providing firewood and tiles for Zhaoling). This land, as its name indicates, was supposed to supply firewood and clay for tiles to Zhaoling, but, in fact, officials of the Sanling settled many Han peasants there as tenants and collected annual rents from them.[44]

According to this document, the Zhang family actually controlled a large section of these lands. A land register of Zhaoling yaochai guandiandi confirms that Zhang Rong and Zhang Huanbai, Zhang Rong's elder brother, held more than 2,000 *mu* of the land at the end of the Qing. At the beginning of the Republican period, Zhang Huanbai tried to sell the land he controlled to two Japanese businessmen, Nishimiya Fusajirō and Kodera Sōkichi. Nishimiya and Kodera were leading figures in the Japanese business world of Fengtian in those days, managing farms for wetland rice and processing factories for agricultural products. However, since selling land to foreigners was illegal at that time, the Fengtian provincial government prosecuted Zhang Huanbai. This document certifies that the Zhang family actually controlled a parcel of the Sanling.

In light of cases such as this one, it is clear that by the end of the Qing several of the powerful landlords in Fengtian were Han bannermen. As we have observed, this group functioned as pseudo-landlords in local villages during the Qing, controlling huge areas of official land. When that land was sold off, these men naturally took advantage of their option to purchase the lands they had managed. It is reasonable to suppose that influential Han bannermen such as Yuan Jinkai, Tian Yugong, Ling Yunge, and Zhang Jinshan acquired full ownership of their lands through this process. Some of them, now legal landlords, came to form the core of the Fengtian local elite, where they were perfectly positioned to move from local affairs into provincial politics.

CHAPTER 3

Local Elite Participation in Fengtian Provincial Politics

Decentralization of Power

During China's imperial period, the dynasties prohibited officials from holding office in their native provinces. Most bureaucrats came from locally influential families, since only wealthy families could afford to educate their sons for the civil service examinations. By enforcing the *benji huibi* (rule of avoidance) regulation, the central government could prevent local authorities from developing close personal relations with the local elite, thereby minimizing misconduct and corruption.[1]

The rule of avoidance was applied generally to Qing local officials. Officials dispatched to Fengtian Province at the end of the Qing period were no exception, and posts of provincial authority such as the governor-general, chief secretaries of provincial departments, and county magistrates were given to officials who were not Fengtian natives (Table 8). The provincial government thus functioned as an arm of the centralized administrative system of the Qing dynasty.

By the time of the Zhang Zuolin regime, however, Fengtian natives occupied most offices in the provincial government, in line with the popular slogan *Fengren zhi Feng*—Fengtian natives should govern Fengtian Province (Table 9).[2] The regimes of Zhang Zuolin and his son Zhang Xueliang were supported by officials who believed in and benefited from this practice, and some of these officials later played an important role in the founding of Manzhouguo. Many of these local bureaucrats came from influential Fengtian families. That this was the case raises several questions. When and how did the local elite organize themselves into a local bureaucracy and come to participate in provincial politics? How did they manage to drive out the officials sent from the central government in Beijing? In other words, why did the centralized Qing administration system collapse in Fengtian Province and by what process did decentralized political power emerge?

Table 8. High Officials in the Fengtian Provincial Government and Their Native Provinces, 1910–1911

Position	December 1910	August 1911
Governor-general	Xiliang (Mongolian Bannerman)	Zhao Erxun (Han Bannerman)
Secretary General of		
Foreign Affairs	Han Guojun (Jiangsu)	Han Guojun (Jiangsu)
Civil Affairs	Zhang Yuanqi (Fujian)	Zhang Yuanqi (Fujian)
Finance	Qi Futian (Shuntian)	Zhu Zhongqi (Anhui)
Education	Lu Jing (Hubei)	Lu Jing (Hubei)
Law	Wu Fang (Jiangxi)	Wu Fang (Jiangxi)
Judiciary	Xu Shiying (Anhui)	Xu Shiying (Anhui)
Prosecution	Wang Shijie (Zhejiang)	Wang Shijie (Zhejiang)
Salt Monopoly	Xiong Xiling (Hunan)	Xiong Xiling (Hunan)
Business	Zhao You (Shanxi)	Xiao Yingchun (Yunnan)
Governor of the Military District in		
Jinxin and Yinkou	Zhou Changling (Guangdong)	Zhou Changling (Guangdong)
Taochang		
Fenghuang	Zhao Chenyi (Shuntian)	Yu Mingyi (Zhejiang)
Linchanghai		

Sources: Dongfang zazhi, "Xuangtong 2 nian 11 yue zhiguan biao" (Xuangtong 2 *nian* 12 *yue*); *Dongfang zazhi*, "Xuangtong 3 nian 7 yue zhiguan biao" (Xuangtong 3 *nian* 7 *yue*); *Fengtian tongzhi, juan* 135, "Zhiguan 14, biao 11," 49–53. Reprint, vol. 3, 3081–83 (Shenyang: Gujiu shudian, 1983).

It was in the first decade of the twentieth century that many locally influential figures assumed greater prominence in Fengtian Province. Some of them had been elected to the Provincial Assembly, and in that body they began to formally engage in local politics. At the time of the 1911 Revolution, violent anti-Qing agitation led by the Revolutionary Alliance (Tongmenghui) threatened the Fengtian provincial authorities, as it did those of other provinces. The officials of the province were unable to maintain law and order by themselves, so they invited local elites, such as members of the Provincial Assembly, to participate in provincial administration. These influential members of the local community hierarchy won key posts in the

Society to Preserve Public Security, a provisional organization under the provincial government, and worked alongside the Qing officials. This development, also seen in other Chinese provinces at the time, negated the Qing regulation prohibiting officials from holding posts in their native provinces and marked progress toward realizing the *Fengren zhi Feng* ideal. The modern history of Fengtian serves as a model from which we can clearly trace the gradual decentralization of power. In this chapter, I will examine how the Fengtian elite organized themselves into a group of local politicians that attained power in provincial politics.

Table 9. High Officials in the Fengtian Provincial Government under the Zhang Zuolin Regime, 1928

Position	Name (Native Province)
Governor-general	Zhang Zuolin (Fengtian)
General of Eastern Border	Ma Longtan (Zhili)
Governor	Liu Shangqing (Fengtian)
Secretary General of	
Internal Affairs	Guan Dingbao (Fengtian)
Finance	Wang Yongjiang (Fengtian)
Education	Xing Yanshu (Fengtian)
Business	Zhang Zhihan (Fengtian)
Police	Wang Jiaxian (Fengtian)
Foreign Affairs	Gao Qinghe (Fengtian)
Salt Monopoly	Zhai Wenxuan (Heilongjiang)
Prosecution	Zhao Tiqing (Zhili)
Director of	
Shanhai guan	Meng Zhaohan (Shandong)
Liaoshen district	Tong Zhaoyuan (Fengtian)
Dongbian district	Bing Kehuang (Fengtian)
Taochang district	Zhan Dichen (Heilongjiang)

Source: Liu Shoulin, *Xinhai yihou shiqi nian zhiguan nianbiao* (Beijing: Zhonghua shuju, 1960), 260.

Reform Programs in Fengtian after The Russo-Japanese War

The year 1905 is often considered a turning point for the Qing dynasty. It was both the year the traditional examination system was abolished[3] and the year the Empress Dowager decided to have foreign constitutional monarchies researched, apparently with a view to adopting a constitution for China. The five Qing ministers that Wu Yue and Zhang Rong tried to assassinate were dispatched to the West for this purpose. In September 1906, shortly after the return of this constitutional mission, the Qing government announced that a constitution and a series of administrative reforms were being drawn up. These initiatives marked the beginning of change in the administrative system of China.

Japan's 1905 triumph over Russia certainly stimulated this reform process;[4] furthermore, the war had left southern Manchuria under Japanese influence. In light of the severe disruption of Manchurian society resulting first from Russian occupation during the Boxer Rebellion and then from Japanese and Russian occupations following the Russo-Japanese War, the Qing government had become very sensitive to the need to reestablish its authority in Manchuria, and so it embarked on the reform of the Manchurian administrative system.[5]

In 1907, the office of the Shengjing Military Governor was abolished, and the Qing appointed Xu Shichang to be the first governor-general of the Three Eastern Provinces. This signaled the abandonment of military administration over the area, although the banner offices continued to be partly functional.[6] By establishing civil administration over the region, the Qing asserted its view that Manchuria was an indispensable part of China. Xu Shichang set about establishing the new administrative system. In his voluminous record, the *Dongsansheng zhenglüe*, Xu reveals his understanding of Manchurian problems and his notion of government. According to these documents, Xu intended to reform the political, economic, and social systems by introducing changes in various areas: the police, administration, education, and commerce.[7] Xu Shichang's policy goals were incorporated into the programs of the second and third governors-general, Xiliang and Zhao Erxun. These efforts to establish a new political and social system continued up until the 1911 Revolution.

Starting in 1907, under the new civil administration, Fengtian was governed by nine provincial departments: civil affairs, education, law, foreign affairs, finance, the salt monopoly, agriculture/industry/commerce, prosecution, and judicature.[8] In addition, two civilian officials controlled the four military districts, and more than forty appointed county magistrates governed at the local level.[9] Of the high officials who took office in the provincial government at the end of the Qing only Zhao Erxun was a Fengtian native. Thus, the following question arises: Was it possible for officials from other provinces to effectively regain control of Fengtian's local society? This problem, rooted in the "avoidance" regulation, was especially acute in Fengtian, where the administration was verging on collapse after the Russian and Japanese occupations.

After the war the Portsmouth Treaty leased the southern part of the Liaodong Peninsula (Kantō-shū) to Japan. Japanese and Russian authorities controlled the Southern Manchurian Railroad and the Eastern China Railroad, respectively. In each case, foreign control extended to specified lands attached to the railways. By this time, the hierarchy of banner offices no longer functioned fully and the local civil offices were limited to governing only the cities and towns.

Faced with this problem, the Qing government adopted two policies. The first was to train officials specifically for the administration of Fengtian Province. The Qing tried to foster close relations between those officials and the areas of their appointment, while still hewing to the avoidance rule. Thus, they rotated officials dispatched from Beijing around various posts in Fengtian so that they would become well informed about the local situation. The second policy, also adopted in other parts of China at the time, organized local elites into self-governing institutions—provincial assemblies (*ziyiju*) and two types of countywide assemblies (*yishihui* and *dongshihui*). The dynasty expected these assemblies to function as consultants to the provincial and local administrations, and the cooperation of local elites was seen as essential to the effective rule of the Fengtian provincial government. In other words, the basic principle of this policy was to integrate local power into the centralized administrative system.

For centuries, Chinese intellectuals had discussed the merits and demerits of centralized and decentralized systems of power. The key issue was often some upshot of the avoidance rule. Masubuchi Tatsuo discusses one example in detail. Gu Yanwu (1613–1682), a famous intellectual of the mid-seventeenth century, acknowledging the fact that provincial officials of the Ming dared not defend their appointed districts from rebellions or invasion by the Qing army, argued that natives should be appointed to official posts in their own districts because they would be committed to the affairs of their homelands. Gu stressed that in order to realize a harmonious relation between the nation's administrative system and local power, an element of decentralization (*fengjian*) should be integrated into the principle of the centralization of power (*junxian*).

Feng Guifen (1809–1874) supported Gu's policy when the Taiping Rebellion brought Chinese society to a state of disorder. Feng was a leading bureaucrat of the Modernization Movement (Yangwu yundong) in the late nineteenth century. He led a local militia in his hometown, Suzhou, at the time of the Taiping Rebellion and realized that cooperation of the local elite was essential for the reestablishment of effective control by the Qing administration. Kang Youwei (1858–1927), a leader of the Hundred Days Reform in 1898, also advocated parliamentarianism citing Gu's argument. He thought that even though parliamentarianism itself was a product of the Western world, its spirit was historically esteemed by Chinese in the sense that this system made possible the introduction of local power into the official administration.[10]

At the beginning of the twentieth century, the Qing government sought to integrate local power into its administrative system to reestablish firm control, not only over Manchuria, but also over the whole of China proper. And local elites themselves welcomed the establishment of these self-governing institutions as an opportunity to strengthen their political power.

Qing Officials in the Fengtian Provincial Government

The ability of a provincial governor to control his appointed province largely depended upon the governing ability of his subordinates, such as the county magistrates. Therefore, governors-general were eager to retain men of ability in their provincial administrations. Simply put, provincial governors had to have officials who were abreast of the actual situation in the local areas. According to one Qing regulation, a provincial governor could request that the Ministry of Personnel (*libu*) appoint a particular official to a specific office in his administration. This procedure was called *tidiao*.[11] In fact, some officials were able to hold various local offices in Fengtian Province sequentially. Through this system such men began to specialize in the governing of local areas. Fengtian's local gazetteers are rich with examples.

Noteworthy among the bureaucrats who specialized in governing local areas of Fengtian Province at the end of the Qing period are Tan Guangqing,

Zhang Xiluan (1835–1922), Zhang Chenyi (1875–?), and Rong Hou (Table 10). Tan Guangqing, a native of Guangzhou Province, held several offices in Fengtian's local administration during the Guangxu period (1875–1908). He was a favorite of the Shengjing military governor Qing Yu (?–1894) and was appointed to a string of offices. While subprefectural magistrate of the coast guard in Jinzhou, he rendered distinguished service by protecting residents during the Sino-Japanese War.[12]

Zhang Xiluan, a native of Zhejiang Province, was sent to Fengtian in 1875 to suppress bandits. For his accomplishments, the Qing dynasty appointed him acting magistrate of Tonghua County in 1877. He then held a number of offices in Fengtian over more than thirty years. As military superintendent of eastern Fengtian, he rendered distinguished service in the defense of residents during the Russo-Japanese War and was instrumental in establishing the Andong maritime customs.[13] Zhang Chenyi, a native of Jiangsu Province and departmental magistrate of Ningyuan, was also responsible for protecting residents during the Russo-Japanese War. He was rewarded by appointments to successive terms as county magistrate in Fengtian.[14]

Rong Hou, a Manchu Bordered Blue Bannerman from Beijing, was at first appointed an official (*qianshi*) in the Fengtian Bureau of Banner Affairs (Fengtian qiwusi) in 1908. He was later made a prefect (*zhifu*) in Jinzhou and was engaged in the disposition of the Jinzhou manors, discussed in the previous chapter. Regarded as a specialist in the financial affairs of the Fengtian provincial government, he became commissioner of Fengtian Financial Affairs Office (*qingli caizheng guanliguan*) then director of the Fengtian mint (*zaobichang zongban*).[15] Other examples include, Shi Jichang (1868–1923), Tan Guohuan (1875–?), and Zhang Yuanqi (1860–?), who served as officials governing various districts in Fengtian Province at the end of the Qing.[16]

Zhao Erxun was another bureaucrat who specialized in governing Fengtian Province. He was appointed Shengjing military governor in 1905 and left when the post was abolished in 1907. After holding the posts of governor-general in Huguang (Hunan and Hubei) and Sichuan, in 1911 he was once again transferred, this time to the governor-generalship of the Three Eastern Provinces. In other words, he took the highest positions available in the Manchurian administration during the chaos following the Russo-Japanese War

Table 10. Officials Administering Fengtian Province at the End of the Qing

Name (Native district, home banner, degree)	**Position in Fengtian Province**
Tan Guangqing (Guangzhou, Han Plain White Bannerman)	County Magistrate (*zhixian*) of Chengde (1878) County Magistrate of Haicheng County Magistrate of Guangning Subprefectural Magistrate of Securing of the People (*fumin tongzhi*) in Xinmin County Magistrate of Chengde Subprefectural Magistrate of the Coast Guard (*haifang tongzhi*) in Jinzhou Subprefectural Magistrate of Military Province (*junliang tongzhi*) in Fengtai Subprefectural Magistrate of the Coast Guard in Yingkou County Magistrate of Gaiping Departmental Magistrate (*zhizhou*) in Ningyuan Subprefectural Magistrate of the Coast Guard in Jinzhou
Zhang Xiluan (Zhejiang Province, *jiansheng*)	Acting County Magistrate of Tonghua County Magistrate of Jinxian Subprefectural Magistrate (*tongzhi*) of Fenghuang Tax Superintendant (*shiwu jiandu*) in Zhongjiang Military Superindendent (*bingbeidao*) of Eastern Fengtian Financial superindendent (*duzhishi*) of Fengtian
Zhang Chenyi (Jiangsu Province, *jinshi*)	Subprefectural Magistrate of the Coast Guard in Jinzhou Department Magistrate of Ningyuan County Magistrate of Hailong County Magistrate of Jinzhou County Magistrate of Ningyuan County Magistrate of Tieling County Magistrate of Xingren
Rong Hou (Manchu Bordered Blue Bannerman)	Official (*qianshi*) in the Fengtian Bureau of Banner Affairs Prefect (*zhifu*) in Jinzhou Commissioner of Fengtian Financial Affairs (*qingli caizheng guanliguan*) Director of the Fengtian Mint (*Fengtian zaobichang zongban*)

Source: Fengtian tongzhi, juan 141, 46, 51–52: Reprint, vol. 3, 3246, 3248–49 (Shenyang: Gujiu shudian, 1983); Gaimushō jyōhō-bu, *Gendai shina jinmeikan* (Tokyo, 1924), 168–69, 833

and the 1911 Revolution.[17] As mentioned in chapter 1, despite the existence of the rule of avoidance, Han bannermen could be appointed to local posts in their native province because their registered domiciles were the banners to which they belonged, rather than their native places. This made Zhao Erxun eligible for the provincial governorship of his homeland and indicates that the Qing needed officials there who were well informed about local Manchurian conditions.

The illustrious careers of these officials are evidence of their specialization as administrators of Fengtian Province. Because of their familiarity with the localities in Fengtian, they formed a core group within the provincial administration, and as local officials they sustained a close relationship with the communities of their appointment. After the 1911 Revolution, Zhao Erxun stayed on, but as the military governor of Fengtian (see Table 11). Zhang Xiluan was subsequently appointed military governor and secretary general of civil affairs in the Fengtian provincial government. Rong Hou, deeply engaged in Fengtian provincial finances, was appointed secretary general of interior affairs, and he later became the president of Manzhouguo's central bank. Shi Jichang, Tan Guohuan, and Zhang Yuanqi also served in key positions in the provincial government after the 1911 Revolution.[18] The reappointment of these provincial officials assured some continuity between the end of the Qing and the very beginning of the Republican period. Certainly, without the cooperation of administrators already familiar with governing the area, the Republican government could not have controlled Manchurian society after the 1911 Revolution.

Many Qing officials who had remained in posts in the Fengtian administration did, however, leave their offices within several years of the revolution, with the exception of such figures as Rong Hou.[19] When they left office, the local elite of Fengtian moved into their positions. The Qing officials themselves had organized these local elites and given them political power as the Qing period wound down. Let us now examine how this was accomplished under the provincial administrative system.

Table 11. High Officials in the Fengtian Provincial Government at the Beginning of the Republic

Position	Name 1912	Name (Native Province) 1913
Military Governor	Zhao Erxun/Zhang Xiluan	Zhang Xiluan (Zhejiang)
Secretary General of		
Civil Affairs	Zhao Erxun/Zhang Xiluan	Zhang Xiluan (Zhejiang) Xu Shiying (Anhui)
Interior Affairs	(not established)	Rong Hou (Manchu Bannerman)
Finance	(not established)	Zhao Chenyi (Shuntian) Yuan Jinkai (Fengtian) Wang Fuwei (Hubei)
Education	(not established)	Mo Guiheng (Fengtian)
Business	(not established)	Feng Shaotang (Fengtian)
Police	Jiang Sizhi	Jiang Sizhi (Zhejiang) Liao Peng (Guizhou)
Foreign Affairs	Yu Chonghan	Yu Chonghan (Fengtian)
Salt Monopoly	Zhang Yiting/Fang Shu	Luo Zhenfang (Zhejiang)
Judiciary	(not established)	Cheng Jiyuan (Anhui)
Prosecution	(not established)	Yuan Qingxuan (Hubei)
Director General of		
Shanhaiguan	Xia Xiefu	Xia Xiefu (Zhejiang)
Andongguan	(not established)	Xu Zhishan (Zhili) Zhu Yingyuan (Jiangzhao)
Director of Inspection Bureau in		
Central Route	(not established)	Zhang Yiting (Rehe)
East Route	(not established)	Zhu Shuxin (?)
West Route	(not established)	Qian Rong (Jiangsu)
South Route	(not established)	Wang Shuhan (Fengtian)
North Route	(not established)	Wang Bingyue (Fengtian)

Source: Liu Shoulin, *Xinhai geming yihou shiqi nian zhiguan nianbiao* (Beijing: Zhonghua shuju, 1960), 252.

Election of Local Elites to the Provincial Assembly

Preparation for the Provincial Assembly Election

The establishment in 1909 of provincial assemblies in each of China's twenty-one provinces was one of the more important results of the Qing reform programs following the Russo-Japanese War. Influential figures in the provinces, such as civil degree holders, former Qing officials, and members of wealthy families were elected to these assemblies.[20] As consultative councils for the governor-general, provincial assemblies deliberated on the most weighty issues confronting the province, such as budgets, taxes, public loans, agriculture, manufacturing industries, commerce, public order, and education.[21] Many studies have scrutinized the role provincial assemblies played in the constitutional movements of the day. Indeed, these assemblies were established just as the constitutional movement was gaining momentum, and they played a central role in promoting its further development. Delegates from sixteen out of the twenty-one provincial assemblies formed the Association of Provincial Assemblies (Ziyiju lianhehui) in Shanghai in 1909 and petitioned the Qing court three times between 1909 and 1910 for the early convening of a parliament.[22] Along with other provincial assemblies, such as those of Jiangsu and Zhejiang provinces, the Fengtian Provincial Assembly was a leader in the movement toward unified action. Yuan Jinkai, vice-chairman of this assembly, went to petition Beijing in 1910 and was expelled from Beijing by Qing officials.[23]

The Qing conferred voting eligibility in the provincial assembly elections to only the small number of local elites who had attained specified degree levels in the civil service examination, held official rank, or were significant property holders. Prior to holding an election, provincial governments had to first compose a list of voters. But in Fengtian, the provincial government no longer possessed sufficient knowledge of its land or its people to do this.

Xu Shichang, governor-general of the Three Eastern Provinces at this time, explained the social conditions in Manchuria in his *Dongsansheng zhenglüe*. He wrote that the occupation of Manchuria by Russia and Japan during the Boxer Rebellion and the Russo-Japanese War had effectively destroyed the provincial government's administrative system. Since the mid-Qing many immigrants from China proper had settled and cultivated vast areas of land in Manchuria without official permission, and now Han, Mongolian, and Manchu peoples all coexisted there. Xu Shichang complained that the provincial government had little knowledge of the actual situation in Fengtian society and was unable to administer the people and land.[24]

Thus the provincial government urgently needed to conduct a full-scale survey of Fengtian's local society to draw up a voter list. To assess property assets, for example, it had to investigate the chain of relations in landownership. But who should undertake such a survey? It was impossible for Qing officials unfamiliar with the local situation to carry this out without the cooperation of local elites, who were, naturally, well informed of the actual situation in their homeland and exercised social influence there.

In 1907 Xu Shichang created the Training Institute for Investigative Skills (Diaochayuan yangchenghui) as an agency in the Fengtian provincial government; this was the first step toward preparing for the Provincial Assembly election.[25] Xu describes the features of the Training Institute in detail in his *Dongsansheng zhenglüe*. According to that account, he ordered the county magistrates across Fengtian Province to recommend able young men from each county for enrollment in the institute. About 100 students enlisted from among the local elite received several months of intensive instruction in land surveying, geography, geology, agriculture, mining, economics, transportation, and photography for use in the impending survey. After graduation, from October 1907 through June 1908, these students were dispatched to their home villages. As supervisory investigators, they carried out a census and a broad survey of the land, climate, life, education, politics, agriculture, manufacturing, mining, business, transportation, and customs.[26] This was the first comprehensive collection of data gathered in Fengtian during the Qing period. The reports of the survey provided primary information for the future Provincial Assembly election and also for the subsequent reform programs that promised changes to so many aspects of life.

To build on the work accomplished by its Training Institute, in 1908 the Fengtian provincial government founded the Research Institute for Self-Government (Zizhi yanjiusuo) in the city of Fengtian (Fengtianfu, present day Shenyang), which was subordinate to the Fengtian Bureau for Self-Government (Quansheng zizhiju), established that same year. According to Xu's description, many graduates of the Training Institute for Investigative Skills were subsequently enrolled in this new institute. The student body was also supplemented by new candidates recommended by county magistrates.[27] To qualify for enrollment in the Research Institute for Self-Government, one had to: 1) be a male twenty to fifty years old; 2) own property; 3) have moral integrity; 4) be literate.[28] These conditions meant that only wealthy landlords and their sons were eligible to enter. This new organization educated its students to act as pseudo-officials in the province, officials whose tasks were to investigate conditions in Fengtian and organize local elites in each area for the future Provincial Assembly election.

To achieve the above objectives, Xu explained, the subjects taught at the Research Institute for Self-Government included constitution, law, politics, economics, finance, and business.[29] Students were not given lectures in traditional Chinese subjects, such as the Confucian classics, but were taught practical modern subjects. The civil service examination had already been abolished in 1905, so receiving a modern-style education became an important means for the younger generation to win positions in officialdom. Many young intellectuals were eager to study abroad or in the newly established Western-style schools of the day. For the sons of the Fengtian local elite, admission to the Research Institute for Self-Government was the road to securing official position. The Training Institute and the Research Institute, both organized to support the provincial elections, in fact came to function as training grounds for future bureaucrats in the provincial government.

The Fengtian provincial government then expanded the Research Institute for Self-Government by establishing branches in every county of the province. The institute's graduates were asked to leave Fengtianfu and return to their home villages to set up branches there. They received appointments as lecturers at these county branches and taught the sons of the local elite in their home communities. According to Xiliang's memorial, 173 graduates of the Research Institute in Fengtianfu went on to became lecturers at the institute's branches in their home villages in 1909. The total number of students registered at the Institute in Fengtianfu and its thirty-four county branches was 2,686 in 1909 and 3,785 in 1910.[30] The Fengtian provincial government expected these students to play a leading role in organizing local elites in their home villages. Starting with an inefficient and out-of-touch administrative system after the Russo-Japanese War, the Fengtian provincial government thus tried to win influence over local elites by establishing these two institutes.

The students of these schools did indeed play the role the provincial government expected of them. Local elites responded positively to provincial policies that strengthened their political and social power within their communities. For example, an essay compiled in the series *Wenshi ziliao*, "Xinhai geming zai Liaoyang" (The 1911 Revolution in Liaoyang), explains that in Liaoyang, about ten members of the local elite, which included Yuan Jinkai, Xu Zhen, and Wu Enpei, organized the Association for the Promotion of Self-Government (Zizhi qichenghui) and supported the establishment of the Liaoyang branch of the Research Institute in preparation for the future election of the Provincial Assembly.[31] Earlier studies show that the Office to Establish a Provincial Assembly (Ziyiju choubanchu) and the Research Institute for Self-Government were also set up in other provinces, such as Hubei, although details of the actual process of their establishment is not known.[32] Xu Shichang's account in the *Dongsansheng zhenglüe*, however, describes in some detail the process of the preparing for provincial assembly elections in Fengtian.

Students Enrolled in the Training Institute for Investigative Skills and in The Research Institute for Self-Government

Some members of influential families in Fengtian local society were sent to the Training Institute for Investigative Skills and the Research Institute for Self-Government on the recommendation of their district magistrates. But who else became members of these institutions? It is extremely fortunate that Xu Shichang's *Dongsansheng zhenglüe* provides a full accounting of student enrollment at the training institute.[33] Each district (*zhou*, *xian*, and *ting*) sent one to four people, selected from the local elite (see Table 12). Although its total enrollment was only 102, it is significant that many of these people rose to high positions in the Fengtian provincial government. Wang Yuquan, a native of Haicheng County and a Han bannerman, was one such student. He was later elected to the Provincial Assembly and to the National Assembly in 1909.[34] Some graduates of the Training Institute later became powerful bureaucrats in the Zhang Zuolin regime. Yan Panchun (1863–?), a native of Fuzhou, was appointed director of the Bureau of Finance and director of Fengtian Customs.[35] Gao Qinghe, a native of Jin County, held the offices of director-general of Fengtian Commercial Port and general-secretary of Foreign Affairs, among other posts.[36] Xie Shulin, a native of Liuhe, became director of the Bureau of Taxation in Chengtu.[37] Qin Zhifang, a native of Tieling, became commissioner of the Chengtu Police Force.[38] Sun Xiaozong (1874–?), a native of Gaiping County, was appointed magistrate of Zhuanghe *ting*,[39] and Jian Weixian, a native of Liaoyang, became director of taxation in Heishan and Yingkou.[40]

A considerable number of graduates of the Training Institute for Investigative Skills would later be elected members of the national assembly, the provincial assembly, and local assemblies. Seventeen out of 102 graduates of the Training Institute won seats in the national assembly, the parliament, or provincial assembly. The Training Institute thus played an important role as a mechanism for producing prominent politicians for future provincial politics and it provided an entrée for Fengtian's local elite into future prominence as part of the provincial government (Table 13).

Unfortunately, complete records for the Research Institute for Self-Government no longer exist; however, the *Hailong xianzhi* (Gazetteer of Hailong County) and "Xinhai geming zai Liaoyang" provide us with the lists of staff members in the institute's branches in Hailong and Liaoyang counties and their later careers (see Table 14).[41] Records of these branch schools indicate that they served not only as educational centers for future bureaucrats but also as institutions where the local elite could organize and begin to take advantage of opportunities available through the local politics of their home villages and towns.

Election of the Provincial Assembly in Fengtian

Based on the results of preliminary investigations conducted by the Training Institute and the Research Institute for Self-Government, the Fengtian provincial government embarked on compiling a list of eligible voters for the 1909 Provincial Assembly election. According to the *Dongsansheng zhenglüe*, under the direction of an election committee composed of sixteen provincial officials, the 180 members of the Research Institute recommended 52,679 persons, or only 0.6 percent of the province's total population, as eligible voters.[42] The total population in Fengtian was reported to be 8,769,744 in 1909.[43]

In May 1909 preparatory elections were held in forty-five basic electoral districts under the administration of Xu Shichang. Five hundred eligible voters were determined, and from among them 108 candidates to the provincial assembly were selected.[44] In the following month, the second step toward the election was carried out under the Xiliang administration: the forty-five electoral districts were consolidated into eight districts from which the fifty members of the Provincial Assembly were finally elected. Members of the Research Institute for Self-Government supervised the election process.[45]

Table 12. Students of the Training Institute for Investigative Skills

Home District	Name	Career after Graduation
Chengde xian	Li Yutang	P.A. Staff
	Cui Qingtang	P.A. Staff
	Cui Zhaolun	
	Li Juyuan	
Xingren xian	Tian Yongxin	P.A. Staff
	Wang Zhenjia	P.A. Staff
	Wang Jiabin	
	Yu Ran	RISG Student
Benxi xian	Yan Zhen	
	Qing De	
Liaoyang zhou	Jiang Wenxian	RISG Student
	Wang Chengkai	
	Liu Ba	
	Shu Lin	RISG Student
Liaozhong xian	Chen Hezhong	RISG Student
	Shi Guozhen	RISG Student
Tieling xian	Fu Yuan	RISG Student
	Zheng Pu	RISG Student
	Shi Xihou	RISG Student
	Qin Zhifan	RISG Student
Kaiyuan xian	Chu Guanying	
	Tian Kaiyu	
Faku xian	Zhang Shuming	RISG Student
	Fu Xiling	RISG Student
	Cheng Furen	RISG Student
	Rong Weifen	
Jinzhou ting	Ming Lin	
	Li Yanyi	RISG Student
Fu zhou	Mou Weixin	RISG Student
	Yan Panchun	
Gaiping xian	Sun Xiaozong	
	Yang Weibin	RISG Student
Haicheng xian	Wang Yuquan	P.A. Advisor
	Wang Guangchun	RISG Student
Chengtu fu	Sun Binyan	RISG Student
	Liu Xiwen	
	Li Hegao	RISG Student
	Zhang Xiusan	
Liaoyuan zhou	Liu Maoguan	RISG Student
	Zhui Zuolin	
Fenghua xian	Li Zhonghua	RISG Student
	Meng Songqiao	
Huaide xian	Sun Jingyun (discharged)	
Kangping xian	Wang Zuozhou	
Tongjiang ting	Liu Shiyuan	RISG Student
	Yao Zongshun	RISG Student

Table 12 *continued*

Home District	Name	Career after Graduation
Xinmin fu	Han Guobin	RISG Student
	Jin Mingshu	RISG Student
	Gao Fengshu	RISG Student
	Liu Baiquan	RISG Student
Zhangwu xian	Yuan Qin	RISG Student
	Liu Fengpan	RISG Student
Zhenan xian	Wang Huayi	RISG Student
	Li Yintao	RISG Student
Hailong fu	Gai Tonggao	
	Chen Wentian	
Tongping xian	Zhang Zhuangyou	
	Du Xiequan	
Xiping xian	Yang Peilin	RISG Student
	Liu Huiquan	
Xian xian	Jin Changxu	RISG Student
Liuhe xian	Xie Shulin	RISG Student
	Zhang Jinsheng	
Yingkou ting	Wang Picheng	RISG Student
	Lu Yongnian	RISG Student
	Lu Weixin	RISG Student
	Wang Xizhen	RISG Student
Panshan ting	Sun Shutang	RISG Student
	Meng Xiantang	RISG Student
Jinxi ting	Mu Renrong	RISG Student
	Kui Lin	RISG Student
Jin xian	Zheng Huibang	RISG Student
	Gao Qinghe	RISG Student
Guangning xian	Song Jinghe	
	Lu Zhongshao	RISG Student
Yi zhou	Xu Huanting	RISG Student
	(discharged)	
Ningyuan zhou	Bao Wen	
	Guo Guange	
Suizhong xian	Wang Jinqing	RISG Student
	Li Yushu	
Fenghuang ting	Yao Zongyu	
	Zong Guangyu	
	Wang Ruiwu	
	Rong Bing	
Zhuanghe ting	Li Qichang	RISG Student
	Ying Gui	
Xiuyan zhou	Hao Yupu	
	Zhang Zhu	
Andong xian	Yu Linbing	
	Man Shangqian	RISG Student
	(discharged)	
	(discharged)	
Kuandian xian	(discharged)	
	(discharged)	

Table 12 *continued*

Home District	Name	Career after Graduation
Xingjing ting	Liu Shutang	RISG Student
	Heng Chang	RISG Student
Tonghua xian	Sun Bingyuan	RISG Student
	Hu Minghai	
Huairen-xian	Li Pichun	RISG Student
	Xu Bingyang	RISG Student
Jian xian	Yu Huiqing	
Linjiang xian	Wu Tingbi	RISG Student
Taonan xian	Feng Sheng	RISG Student
Kaitong xian	Zhong Qi	
Jingan xian	Liu Zuo	
Anguang xian	Ruan Guangsheng	

Source: Dongsansheng zhenglüe, juan 6, "Minzheng, Fengtiansheng," 17a–21b. Reprint, vol. 7, 3695–3704 (Taipei: Chengwen chubanshe, 1965).
Note: P.A.: Fengtian Provincial Assembly
RISG: Research Institute for Self-Government

Table 13. Members of the National and Provincial Assemblies and Parliament Also Graduates of the Training Institute for Investigative Skills

Name (Native district)	Elected to
Fu Yuan (Tieling)	Upper House (*canyiyuan*)
Fu Xiling (Faku)	Provincial Assembly (*shengyihui*)
Cheng Furen (Faku)	Provincial Assembly (*shengyihui*)
Mou Weixin (Fuzhou)	Provincial Assembly (*ziyiju*)
Yan Panchun (Fuzhou)	House of Representatives (*zhongyiyuan*)
	Provincial Assembly (*ziyiju*)
	Provincial Assembly (*shengyihui*)
Sun Xiaozong (Haichang)	Upper House (*canyiyuan*)
	House of Representatives (*zhongyiyuan*)
Wang Yuquan (Haichang)	Provincial Assembly (*ziyiju*)
	National Assembly (*zizhengyuan*)
Liu Baiquan (Xinmin)	Provincial Assembly (*shengyihui*)
Yuan Qin (Zhangwu)	Provincial Assembly (*shengyihui*)
Wang Huayi (Zhenan)	Provincial Assembly (*ziyiju*)
Gai Tonggao (Hailong)	House of Representatives (*zhongyiyuan*)
Du Xiequan (Dongping)	Provincial Assembly (*ziyiju*)
	Provincial Assembly (*shengyihui*)
Xie Shulin (Liuhe)	Upper House (*canyiyuan*)
	Provincial Assembly (*shengyihui*)
Wang Xizhen (Gaiping)	Provincial Assembly (*shengyihui*)
Gao Qinghe (Jinxian)	House of Representatives (*zhongyiyuan*)
	Provincial Assembly (*shengyihui*)
Sun Jinghe (Guangning)	Provincial Assembly (*shengyihui*)
Ying Gui (Zhuanghe)	Provincial Assembly (*ziyiju*)
	Provincial Assembly (*shengyihui*)

Table 13 *continued*

Name (Native district)	Elected to
Hao Yupu (Haichang)	Provincial Assembly (*shengyihui*)
Liu Shutang (Xingjing)	Provincial Assembly (*shengyihui*)
Yu Huiqing (Jian)	Provincial Assembly (*shengyihui*)

Sources: Fengtian tongzhi, juan 160, "Xin xunju," 49–64. Reprint, vol. 4, 3724–31 (Shenyang: Gujiu shudian, 1983); Liu Shoulin, *Xinhai geming yihou shiqi nien zhiguan nianbiao* (Beijing: Zhonghua shuju, 1960), 494.

Table 14. Faculty at the Research Institute for Self-Government

Faculty in Hailong

Position	Name	Former and Later Careers
Director	Liu Shunze	
Manager	Zhang Shenjia	
Chief Lecturer	Li Yupo	
Board of Directors	Wang Zaigao	Later member of the P.A. (*ziyiju*)
	Du Xiequan	Former TIIS student Later member of the P.A. (*ziyiju*) and of the P.A. (*shengyihui*)
	Wang Yingtang	Later member of the P.A. (*ziyiju*)
	Jin Zhengyuan	
	Zhang Yunchong	Later member of the P.A. (*ziyiju*)
	Xie Shulin	Former TIIS student Later member of the P.A. (*shengyihui*) and of the Upper House (*canyiyuan*) in Beijing

Faculty in Liaoyang

Position	Name	Former and Later Career
Director	Wu Enpei	Later Chief Director of the Central Bank of Manchuria
Headmaster	Jiang Wenxian	Former TIIS student
	Gao Yuheng	
	Hou Naifeng	

Sources: *Hailong xianzhi, juan* 4, 21b–24b; He Donglin, "Xinhai geming zai Liaoyang," in *Xinhai geming huiyilu. di 5 ji* (Beijing: Zhonghua shudian, 1963), 566.

Notes: TIIS: Training Institute for Investigative Skills

P.A.: Provincial Assembly.

Prospective voters were required to meet at least one qualification in two general categories. First, they had to be male, a native of the province, over twenty-five years old, and belong to one of the several categories in which they: (a) had served in educational or other civil service posts for more than three years; (b) had graduated from middle or high school in China or overseas; (c) held a degree higher than *shengyuan*; (d) ranked higher than the seventh degree in the civil service or higher than the fifth rank in the military service; (e) owned more than 5,000 *yuan* worth of working capital or of real estate. The second category stipulated that they had to be: male, not native to the province, but over twenty-five years old, resident in the province for over ten years, and owner of more than 10,000 *yuan* worth of operating capital or of real estate. To qualify as a candidate, one had to be over thirty years old, and meet the same prerequisites.[46]

Only a few of the local elite held a degree higher than *shengyuan*, had ever served as an official, or had received higher education. In addition land valued at more than 5,000 *yuan* was equivalent to more than 200 *mu* of land in Liaoyang, where the land prices were high, or to 300 to 500 *mu* in other areas.[47] At that time, 20-30 *mu* of land was necessary for a family with four to five members to be self-sufficient.[48] The qualifications thus restricted voters and candidates to only a very small number of former officials, powerful landlords, and successful merchants.

So who were the fifty elected members of the Provincial Assembly? Table 15 lists the Provincial Assembly members, their ages at the time of the election, their home districts, and their degree in the civil service examination. Some members, such as Wang Yuquan and Yan Panchun, were former students at the Training Institute for Investigative Skills. They worked on the preparations for the election and were themselves finally elected to the Provincial Assembly. The fifty members of the Provincial Assembly were delegates from Fengtian's local communities. Yuan Jinkai and Xu Zhen (1849–?), the subjects of chapter 4, were elected from Liaoyang where they were local leaders. Zhang Huanyu, a relative of Zhang Rong, and Liu Donglang (1856–1935?) gained renown as the sons of powerful landlords in Fushun and Tieling, respectively.[49]

Table 15. Members of the Fengtian Provincial Assembly, 1909

Name	Age at Election	Native District	Degree in the Civil Service Examination
Wu Jinglian	37	Ningyuan	*juren*
Sun Baikui	46	Chengde	*jinshi*
Yuan Jinkai	40	Liaoyang	*suigong*
Chen Yingzhou	43	Tieling	*juren*
Mao Chunlin	38	Fayuan	*fusheng*
Wen Guangtai	52	Yizhou	*zengsheng*
Yong Zhen	43	Liaoyang	*fagong*
Shu Ming	37	Kaiyuan	*fusheng*
Liu Xingjia	31	Changtu	
Zheng Chengjiu	52	Liuzhong	*suigong*
Wang Xiangshan	50	Andong	*zengsheng*
Mou Weixin	32	Fuzhou	
Wu Guozhen	56	Yizhou	*jinshi*
Wang Yintang	37	Hailong	*bingsheng*
Wang Huayi	39	Zhenan	*fagong*
Lu Ming	43	Fengtianfu	*juren*
Wang Yuquan	44	Haichang	*juren*
Yan Panchun	47	Fuzhou	*bingong*
Wang Xingyuan	42	Panshan	*fusheng*
Xin Youshan	48	Huanren	*fugong*
Ma Fangtian	76	Yizhou	*jinshi*
Xu Zhen	61	Liaoyang	
Wang Zaigao	61	Hailong	*fugong*
Sun Lianqi	59	Fuzhou	*fusheng*
Liu Donglang	58	Tieling	
Xue Junsheng	58	Yizhou	*juren*
Du Zanchen	55	Suizhong	*suigong*
Ying Gui	51	Zhuanghe	*fugong*
Ren Shengzhi	51	Gaiping	*engong*
Zhai Gengyun	50	Jinxi	*engong*
Zhang Yunzhong	50	Xifeng	*juren*
Du Peiyuan	49	Fenghuang	*fugong*
Xun Chengzhu	49	Zhangwu	
Gao Yinghai	46	Gaiping	*yougong*
Fuzhu Longa	47	Tieling	*juren*
Gui Lin	45	Faku	*engong*
Zhou Lianchang	44	Gaiping	*engong*
Zheng Zongqiao	43	Kangping	
Wang Wenge	43	Huaide	*fusheng*
Li Guanying	43	Taonan	*wuxiangsheng*
Hui Rulin	41	Zhenan	*fugong*

Table 15 *continued*

Name	Age at Election	Native District	Degree in the Civil Service Examination
Xiao Luen	40	Guanning	*fusheng*
Xun Zhiwei	39	Kuandian	*fusheng*
Du Xiequan	38	Dongping	*suigong*
Yang Hongxu	38	Hailong	
Hua Jingtang	37	Zhuanghe	*fusheng*
Yin Tingzhang	35	Andong	
Zhang Huanyu	35	Fushun	*gongsheng*
Yong Yunshu	33	Zhuanghe	*fusheng*
Wang Boxun	32	Fenghua	

Sources: Fengtian tongzhi, juan 160 "Xuanju 7, Xin xuanju," 51–52. Reprint, vol. 4, 3725 (Shenyang: Gujiu shudian, 1983); Chang P'eng-yüan, *Lixianpai yu xinhai geming* (Taipei: Zhonghua xueshu zhuzuo jiangzhu weiyuanhui, 1969), 248–50.

Even though a large number of the Provincial Assembly members were civil-degree holders, they were not necessarily senior officials who had already won prestige and power. Only Ma Fengtian, Wang Zaigao, and Xu Zhen were over sixty years old. The average age of an assembly member was only forty-five. The chairman of the assembly, Wu Jinglian, and vice-chairmen, Yuan Jinkai and Sun Baikui, were thirty-seven, forty, and forty-six years old, respectively. The younger members, such as Wang Boxun, Liu Xingjia, and Mou Weixin, were only thirty-one to thirty-two years old. We can also see their youthfulness from the degrees they had achieved in the civil service examination. Only three members possessed the exalted *jinshi* degree, and seven members had the office-qualifying *juren* degree. Many of the young members only held degrees at the basic *shengyuan* level or no degree at all.

As Joseph Esherick suggests in his examination of the case of the provincial assemblies in Hunan and Hubei, these young members of the provincial assemblies might be sons of the powerful local elite who had not obtained a higher degree before the examinations were abolished, or they might have qualified as candidates for the provincial assembly due to their educational careers completed in the new-style schools in China and Japan.[50] For example, Wu Jinglian graduated from the Jingshi daxuetang (later Peking University).[51] Liu Xingjia and Shu Ming were graduates of Hōsei University in Japan.[52] And Wu Jinglian and Wang Xiangshan had also studied in Japan.[53] Considering their lower degrees in the civil service examination, we may conclude that the status of the Provincial Assembly members was not especially high from the viewpoint of traditional officialdom.

In previous chapters, I discussed the historical background of Han bannermen in Fengtian local society. According to the *Fengtian tongzhi*, several of the leading assembly members such as Wu Jinglian, Yuan Jinkai, Wang Yuquan, Wang Zaigao, and Zhang Huanyu were Han bannermen.[54] These men wielded great influence in the Fengtian Provincial Assembly, and their Han bannermen origin can be confirmed by the lists of degree holders in the *Fengtian tongzhi* where their names and bannermen status are recorded. There may also have been other Han bannermen among the young and non-degree-holding assembly members whose bannerman status is not evident in the records.

Even though many members of the Provincial Assembly did not have high positions in the Qing bureaucracy, they enjoyed important advantages. First, they had new knowledge. Some members of the Provincial Assembly had participated in the establishment and management of the Training Institute for Investigative Skills and the Research Institute for Self-Government. Six of them were actual graduates of the Training Institute. In addition, some members had studied in Japan. What they learned in the institutes and in Japan was not the traditional canon, but modern subjects such as law, economics, and finance. Facing foreign encroachment following the Russo-Japanese War, the Fengtian local government was in the midst of a major effort to reconstitute its administrative system, and it had dire need of young talent endowed with "modern" knowledge and practical ability.

Second, it was very hard for Qing officials dispatched from Beijing to comprehend local conditions. In contrast, people chosen from among the local elite for membership in the Provincial Assembly were well informed on local matters because such affairs related to their personal interests. In short, these young members of the local elite benefited from a modern education in anticipation of an official career, and from their familiarity with the local situation. Through the Provincial Assembly election process, they learned to cooperate with one another and strengthened their political and social authority in the province.

In addition to the Provincial Assembly, local assemblies and their executive committees, the *yishihui* and *dongshihui*, were established in 1910 as self-governing institutions for local communities. In March 1910 the

Fengtian provincial government generated a list of voters for the local assembly elections as it had for the Provincial Assembly election. The smaller number, 26,847, in this case reflects only the eligible population from the forty-six cities that were seats of county magistrates. The list was again based upon the results of the preliminary investigations carried out by the students of the Training Institute and the Research Institute. The total registered population in the forty-six cities at the time came to 1,231,219; so again only a small segment of the local population was eligible to vote. According to Xiliang's memorial, those voters paid 74 *yuan* 7 *jiao* in direct taxes a year per head, as opposed to 1 *yuan* 6 *jiao* on average for the total population in those same cities. Thus, once again we see the elite bias of the new electoral system. In June through July of the same year, elections to the local assemblies and their executive committees were held in forty-six cities, resulting in the selection of 590 members for the *yishihui* and 268 members for the *dongshihui*.[55]

Elections for the Provincial Assembly and the local city assemblies were held not only in Fengtian but also in other provinces. However, the establishment of self-governing institutions had particular significance for the modern history of Manchuria where the administrative mechanisms of the Qing government were on the verge of ruin after the various occupations resulting from the Boxer Rebellion and the Russo-Japanese War. By establishing the Provincial Assembly and local assemblies, the Qing government hoped to reintegrate the local power structure into its administrative system and re-assert its firm control over Manchuria.

To assess the actual weight local people carried in provincial politics, we need to see the Provincial Assembly and the local assemblies in action. I will describe in chapter 5 just how the members of the Provincial Assembly took the lead in provincial politics during the disorderly circumstances of the 1911 Revolution. But before doing so, I will examine in more detail the processes by which Fengtian local elites might advance their political careers. The following chapter will focus on Yuan Jinkai, vice-chairman of the Provincial Assembly and a typical local leader in Fengtian, tracing his rise to power in the world of provincial politics.

CHAPTER 4

Yuan Jinkai and Other Liaoyang Elites Enter the Provincial Assembly

A Han Bannerman Moves into the World of Provincial Politics

Yuan Jinkai, a powerful bannerman landlord in Liaoyang, was elected to the Fengtian Provincial Assembly in 1909. In this chapter I examine Yuan's background as a Han bannerman and his advance in the world of provincial politics at the end of the Qing period. This will supplement the analysis begun in earlier chapters with a more detailed and concrete picture of how a Han bannerman might rise in the Fengtian political scene.

Yuan Jinkai's career is worth examining, not only as a case study in Fengtian politics at the close of the Qing, but also as a part of Fengtian Province's modern history as a whole. Yuan first distinguished himself as a leader of the Liaoyang militia (*xiangtuan*), a private self-defense organization for the protection of local villages, in the midst of the chaos that followed from the Boxer Rebellion and the Russo-Japanese War. After the close of the Russo-Japanese War, Yuan Jinkai assumed the position of commissioner in the Liaoyang Police Force. In addition, by his efforts to organize members of the local elite under the Liaoyang Association for the Promotion of Self-Government (Liaoyang zizhi qichenghui), Yuan actively supported preparations for elections to the Provincial Assembly. Subsequently, in 1909 Yuan himself was elected to that body. With his election to the vice-chairmanship of the Fengtian Provincial Assembly, Yuan came to wield great influence in provincial politics.[1]

Yuan Jinkai was a loyalist, and at the time of the 1911 Revolution, he assisted Governor-general Zhao Erxun and greatly contributed to the suppression of the anti-Qing movement. After the revolution, he worked as secretary general of the Financial Bureau of the Fengtian provincial government under the Republic. Yuan also held a number of high offices under the Zhang Zuolin regime, and after Zhang's assassination by the Japanese army, he continued to serve in the Zhang Xueliang regime. Following the Manchurian Incident, Yuan Jinkai cooperated with the Japanese forces. In 1931, at the time of the establishment of Manzhouguo, he was appointed member of the House of Councilors (*canyifu canyi*), and in 1934 he became the minister of the Imperial Seal (*shangshufu dachen*).[2] After the fall of Manzhouguo in 1945, he evaded capture by the Soviet Army and is said to have later died in Liaoyang (Table 16).[3]

Yuan's personal history illustrates several noteworthy points. First, Fengtian's local government changed at least five times during the first half of the twentieth century—provincial governments there were organized under the Qing and the Republic, the Zhang Zuolin regime, the Zhang Xueliang regime, and Manzhouguo. Yuan Jinkai held important positions in all these governments and, thus, his career is illustrative of political developments in Manchuria from the early 1900s through 1945. By focusing upon Yuan's story, it is possible to examine the history of Fengtian Province in one continuous flow, from the close of the Qing through the fall of Manzhouguo.

Second, Yuan Jinkai served the Qing dynasty as a Han bannerman. He resisted the Japanese and Russian invasions during the Russo-Japanese War, yet later he cooperated with Japan in the establishment of Manzhouguo, much as his ancestors had with the conquering Qing some three hundred years before. The case of Yuan Jinkai offers a concrete example of how local Han elites in Fengtian society dealt with foreign invasions and the nature of the mutual dependency or opposition that existed between them and conquerors from outside, whether Manchu, Japanese, or Russian.

Third, all five Fengtian regimes depended on the cooperation of local elites to establish effective control over the towns and villages. At the same time, however, the presence of a powerful local force was seen as a menace by the official governments. Since Yuan Jinkai was a leader of the Fengtian local elite and also assumed high positions within theses various governments, his personal history provides an opportunity to examine the complex relations between local and official power in Fengtian.

Table 16. Chronological History of Yuan Jinkai

1870	Born the son of a Han bannerman landlord family in Shanyaopu, Liaoyang
1903	Organized local militia (Banlashan militia) in his native district in the midst of the confusion after the Boxer Rebellion
After the Russo-Japanese War	
1906	Head of Liaoyang East Route Police Affairs
1906	Commissioner of Liaoyang Police Force
1906	Chairman of Liaoyang Association for Self-Government
1909	Vice Chairman of Fengtian Provincial Assembly
1911	Head of House of Councilors of Fengtian Society to Preserve Public Security
After the 1911 Revolution	
1912	Member of the Provincial Assembly (*shengyihui*)
1913	Secretary General of Financial Bureau of the Fengtian provincial government
1914	Member of Compilation Office of *Qingshi gao* (Draft history of the Qing)
1916	Secretary General of Fengtian Central Bureau of Military and Civil Affairs under the Zhang Zuolin regime
1919	Secretary General of Heilongjiang Central Bureau of Military and Civil Affairs under the Zhang Zuolin regime
1922	Offered Governorship of Fengtian Province by Zhili government in Beijing but declined.
1924	Chief Director of Zhongdong Railroad
1927	Chief Adviser of the Zhang Zuolin Office
1928	Vice Chairman of Committee for Public Order in Northeastern Provinces under the Zhang Xueliang regime
1931	Chairman of Fengtian Committee for Local Public Order
After the establishment of Manzhouguo	
1932	Member of House of Councilors
1934	Minister of Imperial Seal
1945	Escaped from Soviet Army at the time of the collapse of Manzhouguo
1947	Died in Liaoyang (?)

Sources: Sonoda Kazuki, *Hōtenha-no shinjin to kyūjin* (Manshū Nichinichi Shinbunsha, 1922), 84; Gaimushō Jōhō-bu, *Gendai Chūka Minkoku Manshū Teikoku jinmeikan, Shōwa 12 nen ban* (Tōa Dōbunkai, 1937), 433; Yuan Qingxun, "Yuan Jinkai nianpu," in *Liaoyang wenshi ziliao, di 6 ji* (Liaoyang: Liaoyang wenshi ziliao chubanshe, 1992), 151–61.

Yuan Jinkai's Background

Yuan Jinkai, whose literary name was Jieshan, was born in 1870 in Shanyaopu in Liaoyang County. His was a wealthy Han Plain Yellow Bannerman landlord family. It is said that Yuan himself held the degree of *gongsheng* (tribute student) and taught in a private school called Fengtian Shuyuan in his native village.[4] The fact that he was a Han bannerman living in Liaoyang is worthy of note.

Liaoyang is located approximately forty miles south of Shenyang on the left bank of the Taizi River, a branch of the Liao River. The city has flourished and declined several times but has always been important as the hub of the land transportation network connecting Manchuria, Korea, and northern China. To those who dominated Manchuria and Korea, and to the various peoples who founded dynasties in north China, Liaoyang was considered strategically important.[5] The name Liaoyang comes from Dongjing Liaoyangfu (Eastern Capital of Liaoyang), one of the five capitals of the Liao dynasty (916–1125). Throughout the Jin, Yuan (1271–1368), and Ming dynasties, Liaoyang was always the base for managing and controlling Manchuria. And in 1621 Nurhaci also made Liaoyang his capital for a time.[6] Yuan Jinkai built his career as a leader in Fengtian's political circles by using Liaoyang as the base of his personal political clout.

In addition to Yuan Jinkai, other powerful figures also hailed from Liaoyang, including Yu Chonghan (later secretary general of the Inspection Bureau of Manzhouguo), Sun Qishang (later minister of the Civil Administration of Manzhouguo), Liu Enge (later secretary general of the Legislative Body of Manzhouguo), and Wu Enpei (later a regent member of the Central Bank of Manchuria).[7] These men were sometimes called "the Liaoyang Group of Fengtian Civil Officials" and wielded much influence in provincial politics from the close of the Qing through the Manzhouguo period.[8]

With the sale of official lands at the end of the Qing period, the population of Han bannermen landlords increased across Fengtian Province, and many of them lived in Liaoyang. The biggest Liaoyang landlord was Wang Chengxian, a Han Bordered Blue Bannerman, who owned over 7,500 *mu*.[9] Yuan Jinkai owned about 500 *mu* in his home village, Shanyaopu. By heredity, his family, which belonged to the Plain Yellow Banner, served the Board of Rites in Shengjing.[10] The Plain Yellow Banner was one of the

Upper Three Banners and for generations Yuan's family probably served as hereditary managers or cultivators of lands owned by the Qing court.[11] It is quite possible that Yuan Jinkai's family acquired full ownership of the land they had managed or cultivated by purchasing it, or they may have simply occupied the land, taking advantage of their position as controllers and cultivators. Regardless of the manner in which their land was acquired, by the end of the Qing the Yuan household wielded considerable economic influence in Liaoyang.

The Local Militias in Liaoyang

With the near collapse of the provincial government in Manchuria during the Boxer Rebellion and Russo-Japanese War, Qing officialdom could no longer maintain public order, and many bandit groups roamed the area. In response, village leaders organized local militias to protect the land and people. These militia leaders included a number of powerful Han bannermen, and Yuan Jinkai was one of them. In addition to Yuan Jinkai, other leaders of the various Liaoyang militias such as Zhu Jicheng, Hu Kuifu, Li Mingshan, and Shang Zuolin were also Han bannermen. Clearly, local militia organizations were of particular importance in the structuring of the local elite and Fengtian history after 1900.

According to Chao Chung-fu's study, from the late Qing on, a great number of peasants and workers immigrated into Manchuria from China proper, seeking lands to settle and jobs in mining, railway construction, and so forth. Many of them were, however, unable to find either land or jobs. To survive they banded together or joined former soldiers who had deserted the Qing army during the Sino-Japanese War and the Boxer Rebellion, forming bandit groups that specialized in robbery and kidnapping. They were variously known as *hufei* (reckless bandits), *gufei* (band of bandits), *honghuzi* (red beards), and *mazei* (mounted bandits).[12] Some of the key figures in the modern history of Manchuria, such as Zhang Zuolin, Feng Lin'ge (later commander of the Twenty-eighth Division under the Republic),[13] Zhang Huijing (later prime minister of Manzhouguo),[14] and Ma Zhanshan (later a well-known anti-Japanese guerrilla leader in the Manzhouguo period)[15] were once leaders of these bandit groups.

All across Fengtian Province local elites organized militias to protect their villages and towns from bandit attacks. A number of militias from neighboring villages and towns might unite into a larger unit if they faced bandits organized on a grander scale. These militias were called *tuanlian*, *tuanfang*, and *xiangtuan*.[16]

Philip Kuhn has studied local militias of the late imperial period in detail.[17] His examination of their basic structure and its relation to administrative mechanisms is germane to our discussion here: Like the local militias in China proper in the mid-nineteenth century, militias that became active in Fengtian Province at the close of the Qing were built upon preexisting "natural" units, the villages, which were already controlled by local elites. While local militias were organized under the preexisting power of the local elite, it is significant that some of Fengtian's elites were able to greatly expand their political power through their organization and command of these units.

The *Liaoyang xianzhi* (Gazetteer of Liaoyang County), compiled by such Liaoyang elites as Bai Yongzheng and Yuan Jinkai himself in 1927, points to this development. This work devotes a considerable number of pages to the description of local militia activities at the close of the Qing.[18] Since it generally describes Liaoyang's local history in a dry manner, the detail and vividness of the gazetteer's account of the local militia is striking and suggests that its compilers envisioned militia organization and their command as a significant stage in their own histories, a stage critical to their rise to power. The gazetteer's first mention of the local militias is as follows:

> In the Tongzhi [1862–1874] and the Guangxu [1875–1908] periods, the Liaoyang border areas were attacked by bandits four times. Small attacks occurred in the year *bingyin* [1868] of the Tongzhi period and in the year *jiawu* [1894, start of the Sino-Japanese War] of the Guangxu period; large attacks were sustained in the year *gengzi* [1900, Boxer Rebellion] in the Guangxu period and in the year *jiachen* [1904, Russo-Japanese War] of the Guangxu period. That the whole area and the people did not fall into total chaos was due to the power of the local militias.[19]

Summarizing the descriptions from the *Liaoyang xianzhi*, Appendix B outlines the activities of local militias in Liaoyang and the areas in which they were organized. The gazetteer indicates the number of villages and personnel involved. According to its figures, each militia unit comprised from twenty villages (the militias of Shaxutun and Chenjiatai) to fifty-three villages (the Xilu militia led by Yu Xinghe). The number of people organized in these units ranged from a little more than 1,000 (the militia led by Yu Xinghe) to several tens of thousands (that of Jidongyu led by Xu Zhen). The local militias of Banlashan, North Bajiazi, and Shenwo were said to have consisted of several tens of villages. Unfortunately, the *Liaoyang xianzhi* does not describe the exact process by which village militias were linked and how the large-scale units were organized. However, from these figures, we may conclude that Liaoyang's militias were organized on a scale considerably beyond the territory of each village.

Many of the militias in Liaoyang were organized around the time of the Boxer Rebellion. However, in Jidongyu, which spread across the mountainous southern part of the county, and the area surrounded by the Hun and Liao rivers, local militias had been formed earlier. Both areas are isolated border regions to which official control did not adequately extend, thus necessitating local initiative in devising a means of protection.

Bandit activities in Jidongyu had become quite a problem during the Tongzhi period, and in response a member of the local elite, Guang Qingfu, organized a militia there. After his death, Xu Zhen succeeded him as militia commander. Appointed commander by Xu Qingzhang, magistrate of Liaoyang subprefecture, Xu Zhen organized a larger militia during the Sino-Japanese War by integrating forces from more than one hundred villages, including those located in parts of the neighboring counties of Haicheng, Xiuyan, and Fenghuang. The *Liaoyang xianzhi* stresses how Xu Zhen's force successfully harassed the Japanese military as it attempted to occupy the Jidongyu area, eventually forcing the Japanese to abandon their campaign. It describes in detail the courageous guerrilla-style warfare mounted by Xu Zhen and his men. The name Xu Zhen was said to have been legendary even among the Japanese military at the time of the Russo-Japanese War. The gazetteer describes Xu Zhen's campaign against Japanese forces as follows:

> The commander of the Jidongyu militia, Xu Zhen, organized the local militiamen in southern Liaoyang. Equipped with spears and guns, these militiamen guarded Hanjialing and Songjialing, the passes to Jidongyu village. Flying flags in the daytime and burning torches at night, they employed guerrilla tactics. One day, Xu Zhen's militiamen lured one

> hundred Japanese cavalry soldiers to their base by beating drums. They ambushed and shot the Japanese soldiers; then the Japanese Army was forced to retreat from the area. . . . At the time of the Russo-Japanese War, the Japanese Army [again] passed through Jidongyu. Pointing out Xu Zhen's house, one officer said that he [Xu Zhen] had fought against us very well in the Sino-Japanese War.[20]

According to the *Liaoyang xianzhi*, during the Boxer Rebellion Xu Zhen again formed a militia several tens of thousands strong and defended his area from bandit attack.[21] By this time, Xu had established himself as a powerful leader in southern Liaoyang and later, in 1909, he was elected from there to the Provincial Assembly.[22]

Unfortunately, Japanese historical sources do not confirm these activities of the Jidongyu militia during the Sino-Japanese and the Russo-Japanese wars. However, there are Japanese documents from the Russo-Japanese War that record a Japanese unit led by Colonel Yasumura Norio temporarily taking control of a village called Jidongyu on August 4, 1904. These documents, however, make no reference to the incident the *Liaoyang xianzhi* describes.[23]

Yuan Jinkai organized a local militia in northern Liaoyang. According to the *Liaoyang xianzhi*, in 1903 a bandit group led by Chen Xianwan attacked Shanyaopu, Yuan's native village. Yuan and his brother-in-law, Su Huicen, lured Chen's men with wine and women. Yuan successfully captured Chen Xianwan and sent him to the local *yamen* (government office). At that time, Yuan was only thirty-three years old. After this incident, he established the Banlashan militia by merging the militias of several dozen villages, such as Banlashanzi and Lüfangsi.[24] Through his command of this militia, he gained control over the strategic area connecting Shenyang and Liaoyang.

It is noteworthy that out of the three provincial assembly members representing Liaoyang, two—Yuan Jinkai and Xu Zhen—had been local militia leaders. The *Liaoyang xianzhi*'s compilers, some of whom, including Yuan Jinkai, were former commanders, had these words of praise for their activities as militia headmen:

> The Liaoyang militias were conspicuous for their courage and strength in the southeast and superiority in wisdom and strategy in the northwest.[25]

These official gazetteer descriptions appear to be deliberate attempts by these local elites to increase their standing and legitimacy.

Local Militias under Local Elite Leadership

Regardless of the militias' success in maintaining social stability and defending against invaders, the fact that members of the local elite controlled these forces could sometimes be threatening to the Qing administration.

For one thing, local militias interfered with the work of conscription and taxation, which should in principle have been carried out by under official auspices in peaceful times. The *Liaoyang xianzhi* contains descriptions such as "[the local militia] requisitions laborers from door to door";[26] "[the local militia] obtains militiamen from households in proportion to the acreage of their land ownership";[27] and "[the local militia] levies 1 *jiao* of additional tax per 1 *ri* of land (approximately 6 *mu*) and uses it for surveillance units."[28] It was not Qing provincial officials, but members of the local elite who recruited militia members from each household and collected contributions toward the cost of managing the local force, and this situation interfered with Qing efforts to assert its centralized power structure.

Another concern of the Qing administration was the ever-present danger that an armed local force might direct itself against the official administration. In fact, some local militia-related groups, such as the village associations (*lianzhuanghui*) in Zhuanghe and Fuzhou, strongly resisted a tax increase imposed by the provincial government and fought against Qing forces.[29] There were also local militia that became integrated with professional armed groups. For example, the Liaoyang Xilu militia, organized by Feng Shaotang, a *jinshi* native to Liaoyang and a famous Qing bureaucrat, included a former bandit gang led by Feng Lin'ge (1868–1925), Feng Shaotang's nephew.[30] These mercenaries fought sometimes on the side of the officials, sometimes for the militias, and sometimes on their own as bandits. Thus their existence posed a threat not only to residents of the villages, but also to the official administration.

The reason the Qing allowed bureaucrats and degree holders such as the *jinshi* and *juren* to organize militias in their native areas was the hope that this way the local militias would operate under the firm control of the provincial administration. In fact there was considerable basis for this expectation. Feng Shaotang, the organizer of the Xilu militia, was a well-known bureaucrat for the Qing, who had served in such important positions as staff of the Hanlin Academy.[31] Yuan Zhennan, who led the Shenwo militia, had also served as a Qing official, notably as the county magistrate responsible for overseeing embankment construction work in Bo County, Henan.[32] Many of Liaoyang's founders of local militia units, including Feng Shaotang and Yuan Zhennan, were degree holders in the civil service (see Appendix B). In other words, they were not only locally powerful figures but also Qing bureaucrats or bureaucrats-in-waiting, and the militias led by these men were strongly tied into the bureaucratic structure of the Qing government

Since these militias had been established by authorization of the Qing administration, they earned mention in the local gazetteer. However, not all militias organized in Fengtian Province came under Qing control. We have scattered evidence that certain militia groups resisted the Qing, and naturally, these were either not noted or simply described as "bandits" in the official record.

For example, during the Russo-Japanese War, Wang Gechen, an important landlord in the Hailong and Xingjing areas of Fengtian Province, had organized a powerful militia force in preparation for the Russian and Japanese invasions. The Qing became nervous about this militia's strength and ordered it disbanded, which it was. Zhang Rong had participated in the militia's establishment since his family—powerful Han bannermen belonging to the Sanling—wielded great influence in the area. Zhang was infuriated by the Qing decision to dissolve the militia and reacted by becoming involved in the anti-Qing movement.[33]

Another example is the village associations in Zhuanghe and Fuzhou. As mentioned in chapter 2, the Fengtian provincial government needed an enormous amount of money to implement its reform programs after the Russo-Japanese War, and it compelled peasants to pay heavy additional taxes. The village associations in Zhuanghe and Fuzhou strongly resisted the government's tax increases, and they were later instrumental in anti-Qing movements in Liaodong.[34]

With the Boxer Rebellion and the Russo-Japanese War, the situation in Fengtian had deteriorated so much that the official administration could not maintain public order. As a consequence, local society became increasingly militarized. The situation was similar to that in the Huaibei area of northern

China studied by Elizabeth Perry.[35] With bandit groups living off the area, local militias and village associations organized across the region. Although all militia groups initially shared the common objective of defending their villages, some retained strong ties with the Qing administration, while others opposed it. Which way any particular group went depended on who had organized it and the actual situation it faced. While clear distinctions were not originally drawn among local militias, in terms of Kuhn's study, the former may be called "orthodox" organizations, and the latter, including the bandit groups, "heterodox."[36] To contain the activities of the "heterodox" groups and keep local society under its control, the Fengtian provincial government relied on the power of the "orthodox" local militias. Thus, in the first decade of the twentieth century, such local leaders as Yuan Jinkai and Xu Zhen were able, through their work as militia leaders, to both maintain strong ties with the Qing administrative apparatus while greatly expanding their political and social influence in Fengtian society.

The Fengtian Elite and the Establishment of a New Police Force

In the period following the Boxer Rebellion and the Russo-Japanese War, once the Fengtian provincial government had restored administrative control over its towns and villages, it ordered the local militias to disband. Since the provincial government had allowed local elites to organize and command militias only where the official administration could not maintain public order, once order had been restored, the *baojia* system—the official system for local self-defense—resumed its function in place of the militias. In confirmation of this point, the *Liaoyang xianzhi* states that after the disorder of the Boxer Rebellion had been settled, the *baojia* network was reorganized in Liaoyang's villages under the county magistrate.[37]

In addition, the police force (*xunjing*) being organized as a part of the reform programs began to play a growing role in maintaining public order in Fengtian Province. According to the *Dongsansheng zhenglüe*, a full-scale policing system was implemented by the Xu Shichang provincial administration after the Russo-Japanese War. The secretary general of civil affairs (*minzhengshi*) in the provincial government administered police affairs in the province as a whole. In addition, an office of the police force commissioner (*jingwuzhang* or *xunjing zongjuzhang*) was instituted in each county and placed under the control of the county magistrate.[38] Governor-general Xiliang stated in several memoranda to the emperor between 1908 and 1911 that the police structure in Fengtian Province was being rapidly organized and improved. According to Xiliang's October 1909 report, the new police system had finally been established at the basic unit of the county (*zhou* and *xian*) by 1909.[39] His report of April 1910 also stated that a centralized police system which employed about 20,000 men had been formed, and bureaus of police were stationed in the forty-seven towns in Fengtian Province that were county seats.[40] In a report from March 1911, a year later, Xiliang wrote that 19,197 policemen had been allocated among the 218 police districts and its 687 branches across Fengtian Province, and this police system was well prepared to deal with incidents during peace time.[41]

We must first ask about the relationship between the reorganized *baojia* system and the former local militias in Fengtian. Unfortunately, the details of this relationship are not particularly clear in the sources at hand. Philip Kuhn, however, explains that both the *baojia* and local militias were organized and operated with close links to natural units such as villages.[42] If this were the case, the reorganized *baojia* system was still likely to be subject to the strong influence of local elites, while also coming under the firm control of the provincial administration. In fact, the *Liaoyang xianzhi* states that after the Boxer Rebellion and the Russo-Japanese War the *baojia* system was organized along the lines of the former militias.[43]

Next, what was the relationship of the newly established police system to the former local militias and to the power of the local elite? We do not have clear evidence concerning this issue either; however, we should note the following points. First, according to Xiliang's report, about 20,000 policemen had been recruited in Fengtian Province by 1910.[44] Recruiting such a large number of new policemen within the span of a few years normally would have posed a real challenge for the provincial government. But since militiamen had played a central role during the war in maintaining public order, it is plausible that these men comprised a considerable portion of the newly organized police force. In fact, the *Dongsansheng zhenglüe* and *Fengtian tongzhi* both state that the new police system was based on the former militia structure in Chengde and Xingjing counties.[45] *Fengtian tongzhi* also notes that some former militiamen were recruited to be policemen after the Russo-Japanese War.[46]

According to the *Dongsansheng zhenglüe*, the Fengtian provincial government founded a police academy (*gaodeng xunjing xuetang*) in Fengtianfu in 1906. Xu Shichang explains that able young Fengtian natives from twenty to thirty years old who were recommended by their county magistrates or members of the local elite in their home areas were admitted to the police academy.[47] About 150 students gained entrance to the academy in its first year,[48] and they were expected to become commanding officers in the Fengtian police force after one or two years of training.[49] These academy graduates, according to the *Dongsansheng zhenglüe*, later constituted a core group within the Fengtian police.[50] Even though we do not have detailed information about attendees at the police academy, Xu Shichang's comment suggests that these students would retain strong ties with their home communities and local elites.

While it is true that the new police system was organized and controlled by the provincial government, which spent an enormous amount of money on its establishment and operation, it is also likely that the police system was in part constituted by absorbing former militia personnel, and that local elites were able to wield influence within it. Although this point remains largely hypothetical, the career of Yuan Jinkai seems to support it.

Following the Russo-Japanese War, Yuan, who had organized the Banlashan local militia and had placed a strategically important Liaoyang area under his own control, was appointed to head the Liaoyang East Route Police Affairs Office (Liaoyang donglu xunjing shiwu), which came under the control of the county magistrate. Yu Chonghan, also a powerful member of the Liaoyang local elite, held the position of head of the Liaoyang West Route Police Affairs Office (Liaoyang xilu xunjing shiwu). Following this, Yuan Jinkai assumed the position of commissioner of Liaoyang's police force (*xunjing zongjuzhang*).[51] If we accept the above hypothesis, we may surmise that by taking an official position as chief of police, Yuan's personal power as the former leader of the local militia would deeply permeate the Liaoyang police structure. Also, the Fengtian provincial government may have given Yuan Jinkai the position of command in the Liaoyang police force because Yuan had already proved he could maintain order in the area as militia head.

As Yuan began to control the official police force in his home county, he was able to foster strong ties with the provincial administration.

The Election of Yuan Jinkai to the Provincial Assembly

The Fengtian provincial government's efforts to integrate members of the local elite into its local self-governing institutions after the Russo-Japanese War were an important element in the province's push to reestablish effective control over local society. As it was, members of the local elite were eager to create ties with the official authorities and ready to participate in those local self-governing institutions.

Yuan Jinkai, as the head of the police force in Liaoyang, also co-founded the Association for the Promotion of Self-Government (Zizhi qichenghui) in 1906. The objective of this association was to organize the Liaoyang local elites and prepare for the eventual election of the Provincial Assembly. Yuan Jinkai and Xu Zhen assumed positions as chairman and vice chairman of the association, and such leading figures in Liaoyang society as Gao Junge, Wu Enpei, Zhang Chengji, Zhang Dongbi, and Zhao Naibi were among its members. They sent able young men from Liaoyang to the Training Institute for Investigative Skills and to the Research Institute for Self-Government; they were also involved in establishing the Liaoyang branch of the Research Institute.[52]

Certain members of the Association for the Promotion of Self-Government continued to hold key positions in Fengtian local politics up to the Manzhouguo period. For example, when the Manchurian Incident occurred in 1931, Yuan Jinkai and Yu Chonghan responded to the Japanese occupation of Fengtian by organizing the Fengtian Local Self-Government Association (Fengtian difang zizhihui) and the Committee for Local Public Order (Fengtian difang weichi weiyuanhui). Zhang Chengji and Gao Junge, other former members of the Association for the Promotion of Self-Government, also participated in these new organizations and cooperated in the establishment of Manzhouguo.[53]

The election for the Provincial Assembly, from which fifty assembly members were selected, was held in May 1909,[54] and Yuan Jinkai, Xu Zhen, and Bai Yongzheng became Liaoyang's delegates.[55] At the first meeting of the assembly in September, Wu Jinglian from Ningyuan County was elected chairman, while Yuan Jinkai from Liaoyang and Sun Baikui from Chengde were elected to be the two vice chairmen.[56] The fact that Yuan Jinkai took the position of vice chairman reflects the fact that he, as commissioner of the police affairs and chairman of the Liaoyang Association for the Promotion of Self-Government, was already quite powerful in the political world of Fengtian Province.

As assembly members, Yuan Jinkai and Wu Jinglian were enthusiastic advocates for constitutional government. At the close of the Qing period, the Fengtian Provincial Assembly was one of the leading organizations in the Association of Provincial Assemblies, which played a central role in petitioning the Qing court for the early convening of a parliament.

Following on the election of the Provincial Assembly, elections for the local assemblies, the *yishihui* and *dongshihui*, were held in the towns and villages of Fengtian Province in 1910.[57] The *yishihui* dealt with such local topics as schooling, hygiene, agriculture, industry, commerce, road construction, and public works. By contrast, members of the *dongshihui* were responsible for executing the resolutions passed by the *yishihui*.[58] In Liaoyang the June elections to these bodies resulted in 16 members being chosen from the towns and 290 members from the villages. The *Liaoyang xianzhi* lists the names of all these assembly members.[59] Former leaders of the local militias such as Yu Xianghe (Xilu militia), Liu Guangbao (Xilu militia), Zhou Shaotang (Xilu militia), Wang Zibin (Liuerbao militia), Ding Chunhe (Wangluotun militia), Shang Zuolin (Wangluotun militia), and Zhao Naibi (Wangluotun militia) show up on this roster (Table 17).

These men, already influential in their local communities and commanders of local militias during the Boxer Rebellion and the Russo-Japanese War, now sat as members of their local assemblies. Unfortunately, the *Liaoyang xianzhi* relates nothing of the activities of these local elected bodies. However, if the situation in Liaoyang was anything like that Joseph Esherick describes for Hubei and Hunan, it is plausible that they barely functioned at this time.[60]

Table 17. Members of the Local Assemblies Who Were Leaders of Local Militias in Liaoyang

Name	Place Militias Were Organized	Local Assemblies to Which Elected, Positions
Yuan Jinkai	Banlashan	Provincial Assembly (*ziyiju*), Vice-Chairman
		Provincial Assembly (*shengyihui*)
Xu Zhen	Jidongyu	Provincial Assembly (*ziyiju*)
		Local Assembly in Jidongyu
Yu Xianghe	Xilu	Local Assembly in Liaoyang *zhou*
		Local Assembly in Tangmasai, Chairman
Liu Guangbao	Xilu	Local Assembly in Tangmasai
Zhou Shaotang	Xilu	Local Assembly in Liuerbao
Wang Zibin	Xilu	Local Assembly in Liuerbao
Chun Rong	Chenjiatai	Provincial Assembly (*shengyihui*)
Ding Chunhe	Wangluotun	Provincial Assembly (*shengyihui*)
		Local Assembly in Shaozhaotai, Chairman
Shang Zuolin	Wangluotun	Local Assembly in Liaoyang *zhou*
Zhao Naibi	Wangluotun	Provincial Assembly (*shengyihui*)
		Local Assembly in Liaoyang *zhou*, Chairman

Sources: Liaoyang xianzhi, juan 23, "Zizhizhi," 1b–8b. Reprint, vol. 3, 869–882 (Chengwen chubanshe, 1973); *Fengtian tongzhi, juan* 160, "Xuanju 7, Xin xuanju," 51. Reprint, vol. 4, 3725 (Shenyang: Gujiu shudian, 1983); He Donglin, "Xinhai geming zai Liaoyang," in *Xinhai geming huiyilu, di 5 ji* (Beijing: Zhonghua shudian, 1963), 568.

Yuan Jinkai's election to a vice chairmanship in the Provincial Assembly meant that he had attained a leadership position in the hierarchy of assembly members. As such, his power over other members of the Provincial Assembly who dominated the local politics of their home districts was enhanced. The following chapter will explore how the local elites in Fengtian responded to the crisis of the 1911 Revolution, how Yuan Jinkai and other loyalists successfully suppressed anti-Qing movements there, sweeping Zhang Rong and his fellow revolutionaries from the realm of provincial politics.

CHAPTER 5

The 1911 Revolution In Fengtian Province

The Rise of the Local Elite in Provincial Politics

At the time of the 1911 Revolution, the Three Eastern Provinces were the last loyalist strongholds of the Qing dynasty. Many provinces declared their independence from Beijing, but not in Manchuria. After the establishment of the Republic, Zhao Erxun, the former governor-general of the Three Eastern Provinces, remained in Fengtian Province as its military governor (*dudu*), a fact that has been interpreted as a signal of Manchuria's steadfast allegiance to the old regime. Thus, in any account of the 1911 Revolution, Manchuria is always considered a politically "backward" area, and consequently little attention has been paid to the history of the 1911 Revolution there.[1]

But a comparison of the political system in Fengtian Province before and after the 1911 Revolution through consideration of the growing exercise of local power shows a significant shift: After the 1911 Revolution, actual power in the provincial administration began to change hands, moving from bureaucrats sent by the central government to influential figures among local elites, such as Yuan Jinkai and Yu Chonghan. By the time Zhang Zuolin assumed control over provincial politics in 1916, Fengtian local elites already occupied many important posts in the provincial government. Our basic question in this chapter is how prominent Fengtian personages, such as members of the Provincial Assembly, began to gain control of provincial politics in the course of the 1911 Revolution.

The Revolution of 1911 in Fengtian Province

When Governor-general Zhao Erxun was informed of the New Army's October uprising in the central Chinese city of Wuchang, he realized that his first task would be to prevent a similar uprising in Fengtian. The Revolutionary Alliance (Tongmenghui) had acquired considerable influence in the two units of the New Army stationed in Fengtian Province in the last years of the Qing.[2] The Twentieth Division, under the command of Zhang Shaozeng (1879–1928) was quartered in Xinminfu, while the Second Mixed Brigade was stationed in Fengtianfu under the control of Commander Lan Tianyu (1878–1922).[3] Lan had been a leader in the Liaodong branch of the Revolutionary Alliance since it was established in 1906.[4]

To check a possible rebellion by these New Army units, Zhao Erxun first mobilized the Provincial Army (*xunfangdui*). In those days, Fengtian controlled five provincial army corps—the Front Route Corps, the Central Route Corps, the Rear Route Corps, the Left Route Corps, and the Right Route Corps.[5] Among these units the most reliable from Zhao Erxun's point of view was the Front Route Corps led by Zhang Zuolin, and so Zhao ordered the Front Route Corps from Taonan to Fengtianfu to defend his administration.[6] Zhang Zuolin, formerly a leader of mounted bandits, had surrendered to the Qing in 1903. His bandit group was then reorganized as a part of the provincial army, with Zhang himself appointed its commander.[7] As vividly dramatized in the case of Song Jiang in the popular novel *Shuihu zhuan* (*All Men Are Brothers*), it was not unusual in Chinese history for a dynasty to sometimes make overtures to powerful bandit groups and incorporate them into the official army. At the end of the Qing, other mounted bandit leaders in Fengtian besides Zhang Zuolin, for example, Zhang Huijing (later prime minister of Manzhouguo), Ma Zhanshan, and Feng Lin'ge, surrendered to the provincial government and were appointed officers of their own troops, now units in the provincial army.

Backed by Zhang Zuolin's military power, Zhao Erxun forced Lan Tianyu to resign his post and leave Fengtian.[8] The Twentieth Division was also transferred to Luanzhou in Zhili Province. Although the New Army played an important role in overthrowing Qing governments in many other provinces, with Lan Tianyu's resignation and return to Shanghai and Zhang Shaozeng's transfer to Zhili, the New Army in Fengtian lost its potential as a revolutionary force. Earlier studies maintain that its neutralization was one of the reasons Fengtian Province was unable to attain independence from the Qing.[9]

In addition, Zhao Erxun tried to isolate Fengtian from China proper. He ordered the suspension of all communication and prohibited the publication of newspapers that reported revolutionary movements in other provinces. One newspaper, *Da Zhong gongbao*, was banned for carrying reports of the New Army's uprising in Wuchang.[10]

News and anticipation of revolution nevertheless soon spread to Fengtian. Many people, anticipating the overthrow of the Qing, rushed to the bank to change their bills issued by the Da Qing, Jiaotong, Hubu, and Dongsansheng banks into silver coins.[11] Anti-Qing movements led by members of the Revolutionary Alliance and the village associations sprouted up in Zhuanghe, Fuzhou, and other areas in Fengtian Province, in response to the revolutionary situation in China proper.[12]

The main force in the anti-Qing movement in Fengtian was the Liaodong branch of the Revolutionary Alliance, established by Song Jiaoren (1882–1913), Lan Tianyu, and others in 1906.[13] In 1911 it was Zhang Rong, a leader of the Liaodong branch, who spearheaded anti-Qing movements across this area, along with Xu Jingxin, Shang Zhen, and Zhang Genren.[14]

The possible invasion of Manchuria by Japan or Russia greatly concerned the anti-Qing movements. The leaders of the Liaodong Revolutionary Alliance in particular worried about potential military interference by Japan.[15] As a result, they hesitated to use military force against the Fengtian provincial government, and their goals instead became securing the leadership of the revolutionaries in the Provincial Assembly and pressuring Governor-general Zhao Erxun to declare independence from the Qing.[16] Earlier studies of the 1911 Revolution in Fengtian consider the conciliatory attitude of the Liaodong Revolutionary Alliance, itself the consequence of the difficult international situation in Manchuria, another reason why the revolutionary movement in Fengtian was unable to overthrow the provincial government.[17] The following words from a speech Zhang Rong made illustrate how anxiety about a possible Japanese invasion made the revolutionaries hesitant to move more aggressively at that time:

> We revolutionaries have already prepared for the revolution. But we have not carried out an armed struggle, because there is a complicated relationship between Manchuria and Japan.[18]

In fact, after the uprising in Wuchang, the Japanese government declared menacingly that it was gravely concerned about the maintenance of public order and protection of Japanese people and their rights and interests in Manchuria. At that time, Japan had about 30,000 soldiers stationed in Manchuria, and Japanese troops in Korea were beginning to mass on the border.[19]

But the strategy of the Liaodong Revolutionary Alliance failed. Zhao Erxun skillfully suppressed the anti-Qing movements in Fengtian by reinforcing the governance system established through the reform programs carried out at the end of the Qing. About one month after the uprising of the New Army in Wuchang, Zhao Erxun founded a society to preserve public security (*baoanhui*) in Fengtianfu, with branches in the cities that were county seats.[20] As will be explained more fully below, provincial officials of the Qing government and members of the local elite such as the provincial assembly members all became involved in this society. In short, Zhao set up a political organization that brought prominent local figures in the province into close cooperation with Qing officials.

The Revolutionary Alliance also failed in its attempt to take control of provincial politics through its participation in the society. Only one of its leaders, Zhang Rong, managed to gain high position within the organization, as deputy head of the office of the Councilors (Table 18).[21]

In response to these conditions, on November 17, 1911, revolutionary groups under the leadership of the Fengtian Revolutionary Alliance organized the Association of Allied Radicals (Lianhe jijinhui), installing Zhang Rong as president and Zhang Genren (leader of anti-Qing movements in southern Liaodong) as vice president.[22] Yuan Jinkai also joined the association as an advisor, but there is no clear information about his role.[23] The declared aim of the association was to overthrow the Qing dynasty and establish a republic. Although it was a composite of various groups and individuals, and its leaders still maintained a conciliatory attitude toward Zhao Erxun's provincial government, it became Fengtian's principal revolutionary organization.

Table 18. Officers of the Society to Preserve Public Security

Position in the Society	Name (Native Province) Title in Fengtian Provincial Government / Position in Provincial Assembly
President	Zhao Erxun (Han Plain Blue Banner, Fengtian) Governor-general of Dongsansheng
Vice President	Wu Jinglian (Fengtian) Chairman of the Provincial Assembly
Vice President	Wu Xiangzhen (Yunnan) Commander of the 39th Division of the Fengtian Army
House of Councilors	
Head	Yuan Jinkai (Fengtian) Vice Chairman of the Provincial Assembly
Deputy Head	Zhang Rong (Fengtian) President of the Liaodong Branch of the Revolutionary Alliance
Deputy Head	Jiang Fangzhen (Zhejiang) Chief Military Councilor to the Governor-general
Department of Foreign Affairs	
Head	Xu Dinglin (Jiangsu) Secretary General of Foreign Affairs
Deputy Head	Yu Chonghan (Fengtian) Member of the Fengtian local elite having strong ties with Japanese politicians
Department of Transportation	
Head	Yuang Liang (Zhejiang)
Deputy Head	Liu Xingjia (Fengtian) Member of the Provincial Assembly
Department of Business	
Head	Xian Yingchun (Yunnan) Secretary General of Business Affairs
Deputy Head	Sun Baikun (Fengtian) Vice Chairman of the Provincial Assembly
Department of Military Administration	
Head	Nie Ruqing (Anhui) Commander of the Second Mixed Brigade of the Fengtian Army
Deputy Head	Zhang Zuolin (Fengtian) Commander of the Front Route Division of the Fengtian Army

Table 18 *continued*

Position in the Society	Name (Native Province) Title in Fengtian Provincial Government / Position in Provincial Assembly
Department of Finance	
Head	Zhu Zhongqi (Anhui) Secretary General of Finance
Deputy Head	Xiong Xiling (Hunan) Secretary General of the Salt Monopoly
Department of Education	
Head	Shao Zhang (Zhejiang) Secretary General of Education
Deputy Head	Zeng Youyi (Fengtian) Member of Fengtian local educational circles
Department of Internal Affairs	
Head	Zhang Yuanqi (Fujian) Secretary General of Internal Affairs
Deputy Head	Wang Yintang (Fengtian) Member of the Provincial Assembly
Department of Law	
Head	Wang Shijie (Zhejian) Secretary General of the High Prosecutor's Office
Deputy Head	An Maoyin (Shandong)

Source: Shengjing shibao, September 24 and 27 in Xuantong 3 (1911).

After its founding, the association demanded the following three concessions from the provincial government: (1) tax relief in response to peasants' anti-tax movements in Zhuanghe and Ningyuan; (2) the restoration of Lan Tianyu to commander of the Second Mixed Brigade; (3) the suspension of logistical aid for the Qing army in China proper. Zhao Erxun immediately refused to meet these demands.[24] After the breakdown of negotiations with Zhao Erxun's provincial government, some leaders of Allied Radicals who headed village associations began to organize their own anti-Qing activities, while others, such as Zhang Rong, still pursued compromise with Zhao.[25]

A peasant uprising in Zhuanghe initiated a full-scale popular movement across Fengtian that responded to the revolutionary situation in China proper. On November 20, 1911, led by such village association heads as Gu Renyi, Gu Renbang, and Pan Silao, the peasant movement quickly occupied the Zhuanghe area. This rebellion was an extension of the anti-tax movement that had been suppressed by the Qing armies in August. Anti-Qing movements led by men from the Association of Allied Radicals also spread to other areas, such as Fuzhou, Fenghuang, Ningyuan, and Tieling.[26]

With unrest spiraling, Zhao Erxun moved to subdue the leadership of the anti-Qing movements in Fengtian once and for all. On January 23, 1912, he mobilized Zhang Zuolin's army and had key members of the Association of Allied Radicals killed, including Zhang Rong. This in effect eliminated the Association. The evening he was killed, Zhang Rong had had dinner at a restaurant named Deyilou in Fengtianfu with Yuan Jinkai and Zeng Youyi, deputy head of the Educational Department in the Society to Preserve Public Security. On his way home, he was shot dead by subordinates of Zhang Zuolin. He was only twenty-eight years old. On that same evening, soldiers looted Zhang Rong's house and that of his brother Zhang Huanbai, doing damage that was reported to amount to 55,300 taels or more.[27]

These tactics effectively destroyed the anti-Qing movement in the center of Fengtian. Upon receiving a report of Zhao Erxun's response to the anti-Qing forces, the Nanjing provisional government appointed Lan Tianyu, the New Army commander who had been expelled from Fengtian, military administrator of Manchuria (*guanwai dudu*) and ordered his army to leave Shandong for the Liaodong Peninsula. Local anti-Qing forces, such as those led by Gu Renyi and Gu Renbang, joined Lan Tianyu's army and gradually took parts of Liaodong Peninsula starting from the south. The northward movement of Lan Tianyu's army and the responding anti-Qing activities in villages and towns in the Liaodong area became a serious threat to Zhao Erxun's provincial administration. At the same time, Japanese interference again loomed as Japan tried to check the advance of Lan Tianyu's army in Liaodong by expressing its concern that Lan's operations might infringe upon Japanese interests there.[28]

In February 1912 the so-called North-South Talks reached an accord and the abdication of the Xuantong Emperor (1906–1967) was declared. Huang Xing (1874–1916), the Minister of War in the Nanjing government, ordered Lan Tianyu to withdraw his army from Liaodong. Upon receiving this order, Lan Tianyu and Gu Renyi withdrew from Fengtian Province to Yantai in Shandong Province, and the threat against the Fengtian provincial government was removed. Zhao Erxun again asserted the local control of the old regime.[29]

Establishment of the Society to Preserve Public Security

With provinces declaring independence from the Qing and the imminent abdication of the Xuantong Emperor, it became extremely difficult for Qing officials in Fengtian to maintain order by themselves. To govern the people and land there effectively, they had to gain the cooperation of powerful local figures who actually controlled the villages and towns. Furthermore, Zhao Erxun needed to make arrangements for the expected end of the dynasty. In other words, to prepare for the political vacuum and the possible spread of social chaos, Qing provincial officials in Fengtian had to set up a system through which decisions for the province as a whole could be made. For this purpose, too, the Fengtian provincial government was eager to secure the cooperation of the local elite.

Local elites were also eager to maintain public order. In addition, powerful local figures (among them Provincial Assembly members) took full advantage of the political confusion to strengthen their relationship with official power and become deeply involved in the provincial administration.

Building on the conjuncture of official and local power concerns, the Fengtian Society to Preserve Public Security (Fengtian baoanhui) was founded on November 12, 1911, at the Provincial Assembly Hall under the leadership of Zhao Erxun and Yuan Jinkai. The troops of Zhang Zuolin are said to have surrounded the assembly hall on that day.[30]

The objective of the Society was declared to be simply the maintenance of public order across the province. Article 1 of the Society's regulations stated specifically that it was established "to protect the lives and property of all Manchus, Han people, Muslims, Mongolians, and foreigners" in Fengtian Province.[31]

The Society was organized as follows: The governor-general of the Three Eastern Provinces assumed the position of president. Two vice presidents, the head of the House of Councilors, and the heads of the eight departments (Foreign Affairs, Military Administration, Finance, Internal Affairs, Legal Affairs, Education, Business, and Transportation) served under the president (Articles 5 and 6).[32]

Branches of the Society were established at each sub-provincial administrative level (*fu, ting, zhou,* and *xian*) and the county magistrates at that time assumed positions as heads of these branches (Article 9).[33] Thus, the Society to

Preserve Public Security was positioned as a merely supplementary institution to the Qing dynasty's official administrative apparatus, as Article 4 of the Society's regulations clearly states.[34] In other words, Article 4 was inserted to assure the central Qing government that Fengtian Province had no intention of seeking independence through the Society's foundation. On November 14, two days after its establishment, Zhao Erxun sent letters to the central government offices in Beijing and emphasized this point as follows:

> The leaders of landlords, merchants, military personnel, and educational circles of Fengtian Province founded the Society to Preserve Public Security on November 12. The objective of this society is to respect humanity and protect the lives and property of both Chinese people and foreigners. The Society selected Zhao Erxun its president and Wu Jinglian, chairman of the provincial assembly, and Wu Xiangzhen, commander of the 39th Brigade (*disanshijiu xietongling*), as vice presidents. The secretaries general of the departments in the provincial government assumed responsibility for the administrative work of the Society. Branches of the Society have been established in the counties of the province, and county magistrates have been appointed the heads of its branches. The Society will deal with all matters regarding the province's administrative issues that cannot be dealt with by usual methods, as well as those regarding the maintenance of public order. The consuls of foreign countries also have expressed their wish to support the founding of the Society.[35]

The Society's basic structure duplicated that of the provincial administrative mechanism of the Qing government, with Zhao Erxun as its president and all departments headed by Qing officials (see Table 18). These men assumed positions as departmental heads in the Society that effectively extended their regular official duties. For example, Xu Dinglin, secretary general of foreign affairs in the provincial government, held the position of head of the Society's foreign affairs department.[36]

But the Society was not merely an appendage of the provincial administration. Former Qing officials may have occupied the leadership positions in it, but more noteworthy are the personnel arrangements at the deputy head level. Yu Chonghan, a powerful figure in the Fengtian local elite with a close relationship to Japanese politicians, assumed the position of deputy head of the Foreign Affairs Department. In addition, Sun Baihu, Liu Xingjia, Zhang Zuolin, Zeng Youyi, and Wang Yintang held positions as deputy heads of the Business, Transportation, Military Administration, Education, and Internal Affairs Departments, respectively. These men were either powerful members of the Fengtian Provincial Assembly or influential figures in Fengtian's professional circles. Among those who held the position of deputy heads of departments, only Xiong Xiling (1870–1937) of the Finance Department and An Maoyin of the Legal Department came from provinces other than Fengtian.[37]

The Qing officials, including Zhao Erxun and the department heads, were given their power and authority by the Qing central government, which was facing imminent collapse. In contrast, the deputy department heads, mostly leaders of Fengtian's local society, were actively involved in maintaining public order in the villages and towns. It would have been very difficult for the Qing officials to engage in the Society's work without their active cooperation.

Yuan Jinkai's position as head councilor of the Society makes this clear. Yuan at that time was the right hand man of Governor-general Zhao Erxun and played a key role in the establishment of the Society. Article 8 of the Society's regulations state, "The Society establishes the House of the Councilors as its highest advisory institution. The House of Councilors is responsible for dealing with especially important issues."[38] In short, it was the hub of the Society. Yuan Jinkai had controlled the police force in Liaoyang and had been elected vice chairman of the provincial assembly. Now he assumed the position of head of this powerful committee and extended his personal influence to within the Society as well.

County magistrates in Fengtian Province were appointed presidents of the Society's county branches under the guidance of its central office in Fengtianfu. As a result, locally powerful figures who took key positions in the central office of the Society, such as councilors and department deputy heads, could control these county magistrates. This meant that the conventional relationship in which official power supposedly prevailed over the private sector was reversed, and as the official administrative apparatus began to erode, Qing enforcement of the avoidance rule also faltered.

Let us now turn to the activities of these Fengtian elites in the Society to Preserve Public Security. Archival materials clarify how they actually came to control the Qing provincial officials and took the reins of provincial politics during the disorder of the 1911 Revolution.

Activities of the Fengtian Local Elite During the 1911 Revolution

A large number of historical documents (*dang'an* materials) on the 1911 Revolution in Fengtian are now located at the First Historical Archives of China, the Liaoning Provincial Archives, and the Shenyang Municipal Archives. Published compilations of these documents include various kinds of reports sent to Governor-general Zhao Erxun by executives of the Fengtian Society to Preserve Public Security.[39] We can ascertain from these reports the roles locally powerful figures played during the turmoil accompanying the 1911 Revolution and their relationship with local officials.[40] Let us examine some of them.

A letter dated November 28, 1911, from Mou Weixin, a member of the Provincial Assembly elected from Fuzhou, reported the Fuzhou area's situation in detail to Zhao Erxun.[41] Mou Weixin was a former student at the Training Institute for Investigative Skills who had risen to power in provincial politics during the expansion of local self-governing institutions. At that time, a strong anti-Qing movement was growing in Fuzhou, and Mou Weixin had been instructed to return to his hometown, Wafangdian, by the Fengtian provincial government. According to his report, Mou led the top officers in the Fuzhou Society and provincial officials in preparing to combat the anti-Qing movement in the area, which had been organized by Gu Renyi and other leaders of the village associations. He reported that three or four Japanese had joined the group led by Gu and that Gu had obtained funds for his military activities from the Yokohama Shōkin Bank by mortgaging his house. This letter indicates that Mou Weixin indeed played an active role in maintaining public order in Fuzhou, commanding not only local elites, but also the Qing officials in charge of administering Fuzhou.

It was Yuan Jinkai, head of the Society's House of Councilors, who manipulated locally powerful figures like Mou Weixin and controlled the heart of the Society to Preserve Public Security. He mobilized members of the local elite and worked hard to gather information on the situations in the local areas of Fengtian Province, the city of Fengtian, and the central government in Beijing. The information he collected and the advice he gave provided important guidelines for policy decisions made by Governor-general Zhao Erxun.

Let us follow the moves of Yuan Jinkai in this period through several archival accounts. First, in a letter of January 18, 1912, to Zhao Erxun,[42] Yuan described information that had been provided by Luo Lianwu, one of his subordinates, who worked for a trading company in Harbin. Luo was originally from Liaoyang, also Yuan Jinkai's home county. This letter reported a planned uprising to be carried out in the near future by "villains" [revolutionaries] in Harbin. According to Yuan's letter, the revolutionaries had purchased arms via Vladivostok. As soon as Zhao Erxun received this intelligence, he immediately contacted Chen Zhaochang, governor of Jilin Province, and Li Jiaao, a county magistrate in Harbin, demanding that they crush the plot.[43] This example gives strong evidence of the extent of Yuan Jinkai's network of information channels, fed by local elites. It also suggests that Yuan's advice, based upon the information he gathered, might well move the governor-general to act.

Zhao Erxun also received intelligence from Yuan Jinkai divulging the identities of suspected leaders of the Revolutionary Alliance in Fengtian. Most of the information Yuan acquired came from Zhang Rong, president of the Liaodong Revolutionary Alliance. In spite of the great political differences between Yuan and Zhang, both of these men came from the same circle of Fengtian elites and both hailed from Han bannermen families. Because of their common background, these two men remained close personally and were frequently in contact.

For example, in a letter addressed to Zhao Erxun dated December 30, 1911, Yuan Jinkai wrote that he had met with Zhang Rong the day before.[44] According to this letter, Zhang had requested that Yuan Jinkai save Wang Shaozhen, a person to whom Zhang was greatly indebted. Wang Shaozhen, a former superintendent of Tianjin Prison (where Zhang Rong had been imprisoned), had assisted Zhang's escape to Japan.[45] At the time of the 1911 Revolution, the Qing police in Tianjin apprehended Wang for being a member of a revolutionary group. In hopes that Yuan Jinkai would intervene on behalf of Wang, Zhang Rong gave Yuan information acquired from a Japanese friend named Nakajima. We do not know whether Zhang's intelligence was correct, but according to the information he gathered, five Japanese under the direction of Inukai Tsuyoshi were preparing to assassinate Yuan Shikai in Beijing. Yuan Jinkai forwarded Zhang's request to Zhao Erxun. Zhao described Zhang's information about the Japanese assassins in his letter to Yuan Shikai and petitioned him for the release of Wang Shaozhen.[46] According to a later report of the Fengtian police to Zhao Erxun, Wang Shaozhen had indeed been released from the Tianjin police station and was hiding in Zhang Rong's house in Fengtianfu.[47] When we try to understand why Yuan Jinkai, Zhang Rong, and Zhao Erxun, for all their political and professional differences, kept in such close contact, we clearly cannot ignore their common origin in the circles of Fengtian Province's locally powerful Han bannermen families.

In a December 1911 report to Zhao Erxun, Yuan discusses two ways of dealing with the anti-Qing movement in Fengtian, based on information he had obtained from Zhang Rong.[48] The first was for Zhang Rong to persuade leaders of the anti-Qing movement to leave Fengtian. Three vice presidents of the Association of Allied Radicals—Zhang Genren, Liu Danian, and Li Dehu—and the head of the Military Administration Office of the association, Gu Tianbao, were cited in this letter as the revolutionary leaders who were likely to be open to Zhang Rong's persuasion.

The second measure was to crush the movement by using military force and protect the Qing administration by mobilizing provincial military forces such as Zhang Zuolin's army. The letter reported that after the meeting, Zhang Rong stated that if the first measure—persuasion—were to be adopted, he would exile himself to a distant place, and that if the second one—military action—were to be adopted, he did not mind dying. Indeed, Zhang Rong was killed by Zhang Zuolin's men in spite of Yuan's efforts to persuade him to leave Fengtian.

It is difficult to establish whether or not these conversations between Yuan Jinkai and Zhang Rong actually took place. It is strange that Zhang Rong, a leader of the revolutionary movement in Fengtian, would reveal the internal affairs of the Fengtian Revolutionary Alliance to Yuan Jinkai, a Qing loyalist. However, it is also true that Yuan and Zhang were on close terms and that Yuan Jinkai himself had joined the Association of Allied Radicals. And Zhang Rong, for his part, sought through Yuan a compromise with the provincial government. In light of the documentary evidence, we have to consider these conversations at least plausible.

When we consider the fact that Zhang Rong and other anti-Qing leaders were later killed by the provincial administration, we can infer that the type of information forwarded by Yuan Jinkai became an important basis for

Zhao Erxun's actions against the anti-Qing movement. Here, the Fengtian provincial government had to rely upon the personal influence of Yuan Jinkai, with his strong ties to powerful members of the local elite, including the local revolutionaries.

In addition, to cope with China's confused political situation, it was also urgent that Governor-general Zhao Erxun keep abreast of the circumstances of the central government in Beijing and of the provinces in China proper. It is doubtful whether precise information on the situation of the central government in Beijing was fully communicated to the provinces in the midst of the revolution. Still, Zhao Erxun needed the latest information on Beijing, and he used every possible means to get it. With his extensive connections Yuan Jinkai was able to meet Zhao's needs satisfactorily. Yuan sent Wang Yintang, a member of the provincial assembly elected from Hailong County and also deputy head of the Internal Affairs Department of the Society to Preserve Public Security, and Zeng Youyi (1871–?), deputy head of the Educational Department of the Society, to gather information for him in Beijing.

After the 1911 Revolution, Wang Yintang would become a member of the national House of Representatives and work as a radical leader in the anti-Yuan Shikai movement.[49] Zeng Youyi later became a powerful local bureaucrat and held such positions as superintendent of Shanhaiguan under the Zhang Zuolin regime.[50] According to "Xinhai geming yu Zhan Rong," reminiscences of the 1911 Revolution in Fengtian by Qin Chengzhi, a member of the Revolutionary Alliance, Zeng Youyi was a close adherent of Yuan Jinkai. Zeng's family had also maintained a close relationship with Zhang Rong's family over several generations. In one episode, Zeng Youyi and his mother sought shelter at Zhang Rong's house when floods threatened the Zeng's home. Zeng Youyi used his influence in Fengtian educational circles to hire Zhang Gui, Zhang Rong's older sister, as a teacher at a newly established women's school in Fengtian. As soon as he discovered the plot to assassinate Zhang Rong, Zeng told Zhang Huanbai, Zhang Rong's older brother, so that he could arrange for his brother's escape.[51]

Three letters from Wang Yintang and Zeng Youyi to Yuan Jinkai, from Beijing and dated January 19, 23, and 29, 1912, cover a period in which the abdication of the Xuantong Emperor had become a crucial issue.[52] Based on these letters, Yuan Jinkai was able to report the situation in Beijing to Zhao Erxun in detail.

In his January 19 letter, Wang Yintang stated that under the leadership of Yuan Shikai, political circles in Beijing were rapidly moving toward advocating for the abdication of the Xuantong Emperor.[53] In the letter of January 23, Wang described in detail the moves against the shift to a republic made by Qing imperial family members, including Prince Qing and Prince Su.[54] According to this letter, under instructions from Yuan Shikai, such high government officials as Zhao Bingjun, Liang Dunyan, and Hu Weide had strongly urged the abdication of the emperor. In these letters, Wang Yintang also requested that Governor-general Zhao Erxun play a central role in checking Yuan Shikai by mobilizing the armies of Zhang Zuolin and Feng Delin. Wang stressed that only the military forces of Fengtian Province could prevent China from establishing a republic.

In the letter dated January 23, Wang Yintang stated that if Yuan Shikai rebelled, there would be no way to oppose him other than turning to foreign military forces. He continued to say that the country could lose a great deal if it resorted to the foreign military; however, the use of foreign power would be better than seeing the dynasty die. Citing historical precedent, he argued that it had not been a wise decision for the Tang dynasty (618–907) to use Uighurs, but that if the Tang had not done so, the dynasty itself would have collapsed within five years. Finally, he proposed that Zhao Erxun should secretly negotiate with the Japanese consul to obtain military assistance that would check Yuan Shikai and the revolutionaries.[55] By referring to the Tang borrowing the Uighurs' military power to put down the An Lushan Rebellion, Wang Yintang was clearly trying to rationalize inviting the Japanese to step in and help suppress the revolutionary movement in Fengtian.

It is not clear whether it was the content of these letters from Wang Yintang and Zeng Youyi that shaped the concrete policies adopted by Zhao Erxun. Zhao of course did eventually succeed in suppressing the anti-Qing movement by mobilizing the military forces of Zhang Zuolin and Feng Delin, and he was able to check the activities of Lan Tianyu by taking advantage of potential Japanese interference as Wang Yintang had suggested. But Wang's letters are certainly significant because they show how members of the Fengtian local elite began to directly engage in provincial, and even national, politics during this period.

As these historical documents concretely describe, during the 1911 Revolution, the Fengtian provincial government depended on the services of a network of local elites as it tried to maintain public order. Qing provincial officials and local elites collaborated in the establishment of the Fengtian Society to Preserve Public Security, which came to be considered the provisional authority of the province. In its organization, the Society seemed to be merely a reformed version of the old provincial administration. However, its membership, especially key members—local men like Yuan Jinkai, Zhang Zuolin, Wang Yintang, Zeng Youyi, and Yu Chonghan—began to assume control in provincial politics, asserting themselves during the confusion of the revolution and continuing to influence affairs even after the establishment of the Republic.

In other words, through their involvement in the Society, members of Fengtian's local elite began to organize and assert themselves as if they were provincial officials. This was a first step toward the collapse of the existing centrally controlled political system (*junxian* system) and toward the establishment of a decentralized power structure (*fengjian* system).

The 1911 Revolution and Fengtian's Local Elite

Recent studies of modern Chinese history consider the Qing reform programs at the beginning of the twentieth century to have played a significant role in the rise of local power.[56] Such reform initiatives as the establishment of provincial assemblies and new school systems, as well as officially sponsored industrialization, produced a new type of provincial elite and strengthened its political, social, and economic power. Members of this elite began to engage in the public affairs of their provinces. Faced with internal and external crises in China, they advocated nationalism and demanded increasingly progressive reforms from the Qing government. Members of the provincial elite became active participants in the constitutional movement. When their interests came into conflict with the Qing government, this finally resulted in the 1911 Revolution.

Fengtian Province is not an exceptional area in terms of this historical pattern. Its provincial elites also emerged and rose to power through the reform programs. They too began to concern themselves with provincial politics and demanded greater political, social, and economic reform from the Qing government.

Under the order imposed by the Society to Preserve Public Security, in which revolutionary movements were effectively checked, such local figures as Yuan Jinkai, Zhang Zuolin, and Yu Chonghan, along with the Qing provincial officials, played key roles in local politics during the 1911 Revolution. Yuan Jinkai and other members of the provincial elite had strongly advocated reform programs and a system of constitutional government, but at the same time they were ardent Qing loyalists and continued to support the Qing court.

We do not have a clear answer to the question of why some of Fengtian's provincial elite were such ardent loyalists. One possibility was that they supported the Qing dynasty out of political conviction, out of a belief that the Fengtian provincial government under the Qing remained legitimate even after other provinces had declared their independence from the court. They might also have considered revolution more a matter of concern for China's southern provinces. In any case, it was their strategy to side with the Qing for the purpose of political survival. Another possibility was that they were guided by their history as Han bannermen. In this capacity some of their families had served the Qing court for more than 260 years. It would be understandable that they felt a special attachment to it.

Another factor to consider is the dual identity of Han bannermen. Alienated as they were from both Han and Manchus because of their identity as ethnically Han and members of the banner system, they became the targets of resentment and possible attack. Such Han bannermen as Yuan Jinkai, Zhang Huanxiang, and Zhao Erxun tried to cling to the Qing court. Of course, it is also true that in the same situation other Han bannermen (notably Zhang Rong) rebelled against the Qing. Although psychological analysis of the Han bannermen's motives in either supporting the Qing court or rebelling against it is unfortunately beyond the scope of this study, it will be an important subject for future studies in the modern history of Fengtian Province.

Contrary to the wishes of Yuan Jinkai, Zhao Erxun, and other loyalists, the Xuantong Emperor abdicated the throne in Beijing. However, even after the establishment of the Republic, Yuan and other influential local figures in Fengtian did not abandon their support for the Qing. By then, they were well aware of their own regional power in Fengtian. In March 1912 Yuan Jinkai drafted the following points:

1. The emperor was forced to declare his abdication. Thus, the abdication of the emperor was not the will of the Qing dynasty. The people in the Three Eastern Provinces cannot accept his abdication.

2. The people of the Three Eastern Provinces invite the Xuantong Emperor of the Great Qing. If the emperor cannot travel to the Three Eastern Provinces, we will welcome a prince, a close relative of the emperor, as the provisional emperor.

3. When the Xuantong Emperor or the provisional emperor reaches the Three Eastern Provinces, we shall form a responsible cabinet.

4. Until the Xuantong Emperor or the provisional emperor reaches the Three Eastern Provinces, offices of the governor-general (*dubu tang*) and the governor (*fubu yuan*) will govern the Three Eastern Provinces and suppress the revolutionaries.

5. The governor-general shall dispatch the Army to Shanhaiguan and defend the border. . . .[57]

This scenario was not realized on that occasion. But nearly twenty years later, Yuan Jinkai and his group of Fengtian elites, in collaboration with the Japanese Army, did succeed in inviting Puyi, the former Qing emperor, to reside in the Three Eastern Provinces. But by that time, Puyi would not rule the Three Eastern Provinces as the Xuantong Emperor of the Great Qing Empire; he came as first regent (*zhizheng*), then emperor, of Manzhouguo, a puppet state of Japan.

CONCLUSION

The Fengtian Local Elite After The 1911 Revolution

Modern Manchuria is often considered a newly developed area because its large Han peasant population emigrated there from China proper in the mid-nineteenth century. There was, however, already a well-developed agrarian society in southern Manchuria, especially in Fengtian Province, even before the mid-nineteenth century. By focusing on the transition that occurred in Fengtian's local society in the early twentieth century, this study has explored issues of continuity and change in that society. A key element in this study has been the collapse of the banner land system.

China used a dual financial system during the imperial period. One part of the system generated revenue for the government (*guojia caizheng*), and the other for the imperial household (*dishi caizheng*). The bureaucratic apparatus of the state controlled the government finances, and taxes were collected and expended according to state regulations. Government finances were thus in the hands of state bureaucrats, and even emperors and nobles of the court were not able to interfere freely with them.

In contrast, the imperial court had its own sources for its private funds. Tribute, profits from foreign trade, farm rents from noble estates, and so forth constituted the main sources of imperial household income. Offices of the court such as the Neiwufu controlled court finances. In many cases agents within the court, such as the eunuchs, took charge of the actual business of managing the court's domestic finances. Some dynasties in Chinese history enjoyed enormous revenues from the imperial household sources. For example, it is said that imperial household income during the Han dynasty (B.C. 202–A.D. 220) exceeded that of the government.[1] Because this category of revenue was usually a well-kept secret, it is very difficult to assess its precise content and quantities in any detail from historical documents. Nevertheless, imperial household revenues undoubtedly provided the basis for maintaining and extending the political and economic power of the court.

Income to the Qing imperial household—as was the case with other dynasties—was substantial. The manor lands and other official land owned by the court were its principal sources of revenue. In Fengtian the Qing court and its nobles owned a considerable amount of manor land, and much of it was managed hereditarily by Han bannermen who were *zhuangtou,* Sanling officials, and other servants of the court. These Han bannermen functioned as informal local authorities in the Fengtian area during the Qing period. The apparatus of the state bureaucracy was excluded from controlling the banner land system since it fell under the jurisdiction of imperial household finances, and this meant that these Han bannermen could gather their resources and cultivate their influence in the area unregulated by the state administration.

With the Qing court's political power slipping sharply at the beginning of the twentieth century, state bureaucrats began to eye the lands owned by the court in Manchuria. With the establishment of a civil administration there in 1907, bureaucrats, headed by Governor-general Xu Shichang, began to reorganize former manor lands and other official properties into civil lands by selling them to private citizens. The local government of Manchuria garnered considerable revenue from this project, and the Qing court lost its rights over the land. In other words, financial jurisdiction over the lands had been relinquished by the imperial household and taken up by the civil government. With the disposition of manor and banner lands, locally influential Han bannermen, such as the former manorial managers and Sanling officials, took advantage of the opportunity to buy up the lands that they had managed and acquire full status as major landlords. Through this privatization of civil land, many former Han bannermen at the close of the Qing period were poised to emerge as leading figures in Fengtian local politics.

Even after the 1911 Revolution, the disposition of civil land, or the transfer of financial jurisdiction over land from court to government, continued. In the process, Fengtian local elites further strengthened their power and control of local politics. This development had significant implications for the role these local elites would play after the revolution. Though the period following the revolution lies beyond the scope of this study, a few remarks on developments after 1911 are appropriate here.

Immediately following the 1911 Revolution, both former Qing bureaucrats and local elites native to Fengtian continued to control the administrative apparatus of the province. In 1913 such Fengtian natives as Yuan Jinkai and Yu Chonghan took key positions in the provincial government, and former Qing officials like Zhang Siluan, Xu Shiying, and Rong Hou joined them. Later, the local elites gradually replaced the officials from Beijing and proceeded to monopolize the most important provincial posts. Thus, we can conclude that it was these same elites who must have constituted the primary support for Zhang Zuolin's regime. Under Zhang's government, the slogan *Fengren zhi Feng* (Fengtian natives should govern Fengtian Province) was finally realized.

Even though it was now Fengtian locals who administered the Zhang Zuolin government, conflict still erupted between official power and the local interests. The case of Yuan Jinkai is again a good example. After rendering distinguished service during the establishment of the Zhang Zuolin regime, Yuan in 1916 assumed the post of secretary general to the Fengtian Central Bureau of Military and Civil Affairs, a key post in the provincial government at that time.[2] To secure his control over Fengtian's local society, Zhang Zuolin urgently needed the cooperation of a local leader like Yuan.

But the expansion of local elite power also proved an obstacle to the regime's efforts to establish a centralized power structure within Manchuria, and so Yuan Jinkai was eased out of his key position into peripheral, honorary, and less important posts. He was first appointed secretary general of the Heilongjiang Central Bureau of Military and Civil Affairs and then director of the Eastern Qing Railroad Board in 1919 and 1924.[3] In the wake of these reappointments, the Zhang Zuolin government eventually ostracized Yuan, effectively stemming his strong influence over Fengtian local society.

After the first Zhili-Fengtian War (1922), the Zhili government in Beijing recognized Yuan Jinkai's hold over the local political scene and appointed him governor of Fengtian Province in 1922.[4] It was an appointment by which the Zhili government, aspiring to national authority, tried to undermine Zhang Zuolin's power in Fengtian Province. Yuan, however, declined the appointment because he knew that Zhang Zuolin remained dominant in Manchuria even after his defeat in the Zhili-Fengtian War.[5]

To reestablish effective control over Manchuria after Zhang Zuolin had been killed by agents of the Japanese Army at Liutiaohu in 1928, the successor regime under Zhang's son, Zhang Xueliang, established the Committee for Public Order in the Northeastern Provinces (Dongbei baoan weiyuanhui). This was expected to function as the headquarters of the Fengtian provincial government. Like his father, Zhang Xueliang invited Yuan Jinkai to play a central role on this committee, and Zhang and Yuan assumed the positions of chairman and vice chairman.[6] The Japanese Army, well aware of Yuan Jinkai's influence in local society, also schemed to make use of him. In the wake of the Manchurian Incident in 1931, Yuan Jinkai and other local elites set up the Committee for Public Order in Fengtian (Fengtian difang weichi weiyuanhui), which served as an assembly of the Fengtian elite and collaborated with the Japanese in the establishment of Manzhouguo.[7]

With Manzhouguo established, conflict once again arose between officials native to Fengtian and those from elsewhere. Key government positions went to Japanese officials, while some other posts were allotted to former Qing officials like Ding Xiaoshu (1860–1938) and Luo Zhenyu (1866–1940), who had served under the Xuantong Emperor. These two men were appointed to high positions—prime minister and member of the House of the Councilors. Yuan Jinkai and Yu Chonghan, both members of the Fengtian elite who had contributed to the establishment of Manzhouguo, were also appointed to be a member of the House of Councilors and secretary general of the Inspection Bureau, respectively.

Once again, it was critical for the Japanese military forces to obtain the cooperation of influential members of the local elite and the local officials who represented them. To do this, the Japanese had to yield a certain number of positions and, consequently, a certain amount of power to local leaders. A 1935 article, written by a Japanese journalist in monthly journal *Manshū Hyōron* (Manchurian Review), described the situation in the following manner:

> At the time of the Manchurian Incident, the Kantō-gun [Japanese Army] sought the cooperation of the local gentry through such figures as Yuan Jinkai and Yu Chonghan. Why did we [Japanese] call on these old men in establishing Manzhouguo? Because these members of the local elite were then actually governing local Manchurian society, and they still are. And they will continue to control this society in the future. Therefore, initially we must form an alliance with them, for only by doing so can we govern the people of Manchuria effectively.[8]

And yet, if the Japanese bureaucrats gave substantial authority to these locally powerful figures and officials, they risked compromising the effectiveness of their centrally controlled system in Manzhouguo, thus endangering their dominance there. In fact, because the Manzhouguo government feared the expansion of local power, it later transferred Yuan Jinkai from his position in the House of the Councilors to the post of minister of the Imperial Seal (*shangshufu dachen*), an honorary but rather nominal position.[9] Yu Chonghan would also relinquish his position. The Manzhouguo government thus tried to deprive locally influential figures of their political power in the administrative structure once a relatively stable political condition had been achieved.

The history of the Fengtian local elite, in particular that of Yuan Jinkai, shows that after the 1911 Revolution, the Zhang Zuolin and Zhang Xueliang governments, as well as the Manzhouguo regime all faced the challenge of integrating local elites into the administrative structure if they hoped to assert control over the land and the people. The situation confronting these governments was much the same as that the Qing court had faced as it tried to reassert its control through Fengtian's emerging power brokers.

APPENDIX A

Note on *Manshū Kyūkan Chōsa Hōkoku-sho*

The series *Manshū kyūkan chōsa hōkoku-sho* (Research Reports on Manchuria's Old Customs) is a basic and reliable historical resource for the study of Manchuria's land system during the Qing period. It was compiled by the South Manchuria Railroad Company (Minami Manshū Tetsudō Kabushiki Kaisha or Mantetsu) between 1913 and 1915 and consisted of the following seven reports:

1) Amagai Kenzaburō, *Naimufu Kanshō* (Manors of the Imperial Household Department), 1914.
2) Amagai Kenzaburō, *Kōsan* (Imperial Estates), 1915.
3) Kamebuchi Ryūchō, *Ippan Minchi* (Civil Land), 3 volumes, 1914–1915.
4) Miyauchi Kishi, *Ten no Kanshū* (Customs of Dian), 1913.
5) Miyauchi Kishi, Ō *no Kanshū* (Customs of Ya), 1913.
6) Sugata Kumaemon, *Soken* (Rights of Zu), 1913.
7) Kamebuchi Ryūchō, *Mōchi* (Land Held by Mongols), 1914.

Manshū kyūkan chōsa hōkoku-sho is a kind of encyclopedia that details Manchuria's land system in a very dry manner and is written in a pseudo-classical Japanese style. It is very difficult to comprehend the key problems described by the reports, which is why scholars sometimes mention their existence but do not examine them in detail. But once we understand why the reports were compiled in the first place, the central issue they address becomes clear.

To construct the extended facilities of the South Manchuria Railroad and its branch line, the Anfeng (Andong-Fengtian) Railroad, after the Russo-Japanese War, Mantetsu (that is, the South Manchuria Railroad Company) had to purchase a large area of land. The problem they faced was determining who the real owners of the particular lands were. It was common for more than two people to claim ownership of a particular plot of land with a variety of documents as proof of their rights. There were also sometimes disputes between public officials and private civilians concerning the nature of the particular parcels Mantetsu wished to purchase, namely, whether it was in fact official or private land. In order to ascertain the real owner of the particular piece of land, Mantetsu had to investigate Manchuria's land system, its customs, and its historical background in detail. This kind of research on landholding patterns was necessary for the company to establish colonial control over Manchuria.

Based upon interviews with landlords and peasants and analyses of land tenure documents covering many generations, *Manshū kyūkan chōsa hōkoku-sho* examines the land system and its customs in southern Manchuria at the beginning of the twentieth century. These reports portray actual conditions in Fengtian society and the landlord-tenant relationship that emerged from the collapse of the former banner land and official land system.

Compared to other Mantetsu materials, such as *Chūgoku nōson kankō chōsa* (Investigation of customs in rural China), the *Manshū kyūkan chōsa hōkoku-sho* has been paid little attention by scholars. However, this series collects and analyzes an enormous number of documents valuable to the historical study of modern Manchuria. It is also highly relevant to the study of modern Chinese history as a whole.

Appendix B

Outline of Local Militias in Liaoyang*

Jidongyu Militia

Period of Activity: ca. early Tongzhi period (1862–1874)
Leader: Guan Qingfu
Establishment: Guan Qingfu organized a local militia in Jidongyu in the early Tongzhi period when bandit activities were widespread. This militia was the beginning of the South Route Militia of Liaoyang.

Periods of Activity: 1894 and 1900
Leader: Xu Zhen
Establishment and Activities: At the time of the Sino-Japanese War, Xu Qingzhang, magistrate of Liaoyang subprefecture, appointed Xu Zhen as commander of the local militia in Jidongyu. Xu Zhen organized a large militia by integrating forces from over 100 villages, including those located in the neighboring counties of Haicheng, Xiuyan, and Fenghuang. The local militia attacked bandits in the southern area of Liaoyang and resisted the Japanese Army in its attempt to invade this area. At the time of the Boxer Rebellion, Xu Zhen again organized a large-scale militia (consisting of over 10,000 peasants) and attacked bandits in Huanggou. The area of its activity extended to Benxi County, the county bordering Liaoyang subprefecture.

Xilu Militia (including Liuerbao Militia)

Period of Activity: 1866
Leader: Xu Changqing

* Compiled from *Liaoyang xianzhi*, *juan* 21.8b-9b, *juan* 22.9a-12b. Reprint, vol. 3, 836-37, 859-66 (Taipei: Chengwen chubanshe, 1973).

Establishment and Activities: Several thousand bandits led by Xu Zhangyi invaded the western part of Liaoyang subprefecture from their base in Genzhuangzi, Haicheng County. Xu Changqing, who lived in the village of Xutuozi, organized a local militia of several thousand peasants from more than thirty villages and drove back the bandits.

Period of Activity: 1900

Leaders: Feng Shaotang (*jinshi*), Liu Chunlang (*juren*), De Bin (*juren*), Feng Lin'ge, Hu Kuifu (*juren*, Han bannerman), Yu Xianghe, Liu Guangbao (*shengyuan*), Zhou Shaotang (*juren*, Manchu bannerman), and Wang Zibin

Establishment and Activities: Feng Shaotang, Liu Chunlang, and De Bin petitioned Zeng Qi, Shengjing military governor, to allow them to organize a local militia. After Zeng Qi's approval, Hu Kuifu controlled the West Route Militia of Liaoyang. Feng Lin'ge, a nephew of Feng Shaotang and originally a leader of mounted bandits, was appointed commander of the local militia in the border area between Liaoyang and Haicheng. He expelled a group of bandits led by Zhi Langxuan from the village of Daluotuobei and also defeated a bandit group led by Yin Lanting and Fei Xiwu and one led by Shiyilao Geju, which invaded the village of Xiaoxidi near the town of Liuerbao. Yu Xianghe and Liu Guangbao commanded local militia over 1,000 residents strong from fifty-three villages in the western part of Liaoyang subprefecture and repulsed bandits led by Wang Zhanbei and Wanglao Geju. Five villages near the town of Liuerbao also organized local militia. Li Yating commanded the local militia there and defeated a group of bandits led by Yin Lanting. In addition, the villagers of Liujiazhuang drove out a bandit group led by Li Tietou.

Banlashan Militia

Period of Activity: 1903

Leader: Yuan Jinkai (*suigong*, Han bannerman)

Establishment and Activities: A bandit group led by Chen Xiaowan attacked Shanyaopu, Yuan Jinkai's native village. Yuan Jinkai and Su Huicen, Yuan's brother-in-law, commanded villagers of Shanyaopu and drove out Chen's bandit group. Yuan Jinkai then founded the Banlashan militia by merging the militias from several dozen villages, including Banlashanzi and Lüfangsi.

North Bajiazi Militia

Periods of Activity: 1900 and 1904

Leader: Zhu Jicheng (*juren*, Han bannerman)

Establishment and Activities: At the time of the Boxer Rebellion, Yang Changhuan, magistrate of Liaoyang subprefecture, asked Zhu Jicheng, a powerful gentry of the North Baijiazi area, to organize the North Route Militia of Liaoyang. In the course of the Russo-Japanese War, Shen Jinjian, magistrate of Liaoyang subprefecture, again asked Zhu Jicheng to reorganize the local militia there. The local militia, composed of men from scores of villages, was then called the Baojia Bureau and later became the basis of the police system.

Chenjiatai Militia

Period of Activity: 1900

Leader: Chun Rong (*juren*, Mongol bannerman)

Establishment: The militia in this area was organized by integrating residents of over twenty villages around the village of Chenjiatai.

Shaxutun Militia

Period of Activity: 1900

Leaders: Yin Xiangtang (*juren*) and Di Chunting

Establishment: This militia was founded by organizing peasants from over twenty villages near Shaxutun.

Shenwo Militia

Period of Activity: 1900

Leader: Yuan Zhennan (*jinshi*).

Establishment: Shenwo's militia was comprised of peasants from scores of villages around the village of Shenwo.

Wangluotun Militia

Period of Activity: 1900

Leaders: Li Mingshan (*juren*, Han bannerman), Ding Chunhe (*linsheng*), Shang Zuolin (*juren*, Han bannerman), Zhao Naibi (*engong*), and Meng Wenge (*suigong*, Manchu bannerman)

Establishment: Residents from scores of villages near Wangluotun participated in this militia.

Appendix C

Units of Measure

The measures below are standard figures. Units of measure greatly differed from place to place in Fengtian Province, sometimes even within the same village. *Shenping* and *shiping* were silver *liang* units that were used locally.

Square Measures

1 *mu* = 6.144 acre

1 *shang* = 10 *mu*

1 *fang* = 45 *shang*

Currency

1 *liang* (*kuping*) = 37.3 grams of silver

1 *liang* = 10 *qian* = 100 *fen*

1 *liang* = 1.7 – 1.8 *yuan*

1 *yuan* = 10 *jiao*

Notes

Unless otherwise indicated, all Japanese publishers are located in Tokyo.

Introduction

[1] The English-speaking world commonly uses Manchuria as a place name. However, it is often said that the word "Manchuria" was a product of imperialist aggression toward this area, especially that of Japan. Imperialists tried to separate the Three Eastern Provinces from China proper by calling it Manchuria. Mark Elliott has recently discussed how the Qing court and the Jesuits conceived the term "Manchuria" in the Kangxi period (1661–1722). Nakami Tatsuo has also explained that the Japanese called what is now Northeast China "Manchuria" as early as the end of the eighteenth century and the beginning of the nineteenth century. It therefore might be simplistic to conclude that it was colonialism alone that established the word as a place name in modern times. See Mark Elliott, "The Limits of Tartary: Manchuria in Imperial and National Geographies," *Journal of Asian Studies* 59.3 (2000): 603–4; Nakami Tatsuo, "Chiiki gainen no seijisei" (The politics of the concept of region) in *Kōsakusuru Azia* (The mutual involvement of Asia), edited by Mizoguchi Yūzō et al. (Tōkyō Daigaku Shuppan-kai, 1993), 273–95.

[2] The following comprehensive catalogues list the documents compiled by former Japanese colonial institutions in Manchuria: Ajia Keizai Kenkyūjo, ed., *Kyū shokuminchi kankei kikan kankōbutsu sōgō mokuroku: Manshūkoku, Kantō-chō hen* (Union catalogue of publications of the former colonial institutions: Manzhouguo government and the Japanese colonial authority of the Guandong Leased Territory) (Ajia Keizai Kenkyūjo, 1975); Ajia Keizai Kenkyūjo, ed., *Kyū shokuminchi kankei kikan kankōbutsu sōgō mokuroku: Minami Manshū Tetsudō Kabushiki Kaisha hen* (Union catalogue of publications of the former colonial institutions: The South Manchuria Railroad Company) (Ajia Keizai Kenkyūjo, 1979); Imura Tetsurō, "Manshūkoku kankei shiryō kaidai" (Bibliographical introduction for the study of Manzhouguo) in *Manshūkoku no kenkyū* (The study of Manzhouguo), edited by Yamamoto Yūzō (Kyoto: Kyōto University, 1993), 535–80.

[3] The following articles are detailed reviews of these studies in Japan: Suzuki Takashi, "Manshū kenkyū no genjō to kadai" (The present state of and issues in the study of Manchuria), *Ajia Keizai* 12.4 (1971): 49–60; Kaneko Fumio, "1970 nendai ni okeru Manshū kenkyū no jōkyō" (The present state of the study of Manchuria in

the 1970s), *Ajia Keizai* 20.3 (1979): 38–55; 20.11 (1979): 24–43; Fujii Masao, "Manshūkoku" (Manzhouguo) in *Chūgokushi kenkyū nyūmon, ge* (Introduction to the study of Chinese history, vol. 2), edited by Yamane Yukio (Yamakawa Shuppan, 1995), 433–41.

[4] The following article is a comprehensive review of the study of early Qing history: Kanda Nobuo and Hosoya Yoshio, "Shindai" (The Qing period) in Yamane, *Chūgokushi kenkyū nyūmon, ge*, 91–105.

[5] Inaba Iwakichi, *Zōtei Manshū hattatsu shi* (The history of the development of Manchuria, expanded edition) (Nihon Hyōronsha, 1935); Ishida Kōhei, *Manshū ni okeru shokuminchi keizai no shiteki tenkai* (The history of the development of Manchuria's colonial economy) (Kyoto: Mineruba Shobō, 1964); Sudō Yoshiyuki, *Shindai manshū tochi seisaku no kenkyū* (A study of the Qing land policy in Manchuria) (Kawade Shobō, 1944).

[6] Robert H. G. Lee, *The Manchurian Frontier in Ch'ing History* (Cambridge, Mass.: Harvard University Press, 1970); Chao Chung-fu, *Jinshi Dongsansheng yanjiu lunwen ji* (Studies on Dongsansheng in the modern period) (Taipei: Chengwen chubanshe, 1999). This latter book is a collection of Chao's articles on the study of Manchurian history.

[7] Thomas R. Gottschang and Diana Lary, *Swallows and Settlers: The Great Migration from North China to Manchuria* (Ann Arbor: Center for Chinese Studies, University of Michigan, 2000).

[8] Roger DesForges, reading his memorials to the Throne, has examined the contents of Xiliang's reform programs. DesForges, Roger, *Hsi-liang and the Chinese National Revolution* (New Haven: Yale University Press, 1973).

[9] Sudō Yoshiyuki, *Shindai Manshū tochi seisaku no kenkyū* (Study of Qing land policy in Manchuria) (Kawade Shobō, 1944).

[10] Joseph W. Esherick and Mary Backus Rankin, "Introduction," in Joseph W. Esherick and Mary Backus Rankin, eds., *Chinese Local Elites and Patterns of Dominance* (Berkeley: University of California Press, 1990).

[11] Philip Kuhn, *Rebellion and Its Enemies in Late Imperial China* (Cambridge, Mass.: Harvard University Press, 1970).

[12] Joseph W. Esherick, *Reform and Revolution in China* (Berkeley: University of California Press, 1976); Mary Rankin, *Elite Acitivism and Political Transformation in China* (Stanford: Stanford University Press, 1986).

[13] Sudō Yoshiyuki, *Shindai Manshū tochi seisaku*; Ura Ren'ichirō, "Kangun (Ujen Cooha) ni tsuite" (A study of Han bannermen) in *Kuwabara hakase kanreki kinen tōyōshi ronsō* (Studies of Oriental history contributed in celebration of the sixtieth birthday of Professor Kuwabara) (Kōbundō, 1930), 815–49; Amagai Kenzaburō, *Naimufu kanshō* (Manors of the Imperial Household Department) (Dairen: Minami Manshū Tetsudō Kabushiki Kaisha, 1914); Amagai Kenzaburō, *Kōsan* (Lands owned by the Qing court) (Dairen: Minami Manshū Tetsudō Kabushiki Kaisha, 1915).

Chapter 1

[1] Hosoya Yoshio, "Manju gurun to Manshūkoku" (Manju gurun and Manzhouguo) in *Rekishi no naka no chiiki* (Regions in history), ed. Shibata Michio et al. (Iwanami Shoten, 1990), 105–36; Mitamura Taisuke, *Shinchō zenshi no kenkyū* (Study of pre-Qing history) (Kyoto: Tōyōshi kenkyūkai, 1965); Kanda Nobuo, "Shin no kōki" (The rise of the Qing) in *Sekai Rekishi taikei Chūgoku-shi* (World history, Chinese history) (Yamakawa Shuppansha, 1999), vol. 4, 295–318.

[2] Oda Yorozu et al., eds., *Shinkoku gyōsei-hō* (Qing administrative law) (Kobe: Rinji Taiwan kyūkan chōsa-kai, 1905–1914; reprinted, Kyūko Shoin, 1972), vol. 4, 275, 277–78.

[3] Oda, *Shinkoku gyōsei-hō*, vol. 4, 275.

[4] Pamela Kyle Crossley, *Orphan Warriors: Three Manchu Generations and the End of the Qing Dynasty* (Princeton: Princeton University Press, 1990).

[5] Mark Elliott, *The Manchu Way: The Eight Banners and Ethnic Identity in Late Imperial China* (Stanford: Stanford University Press, 2001).

[6] Edward J. M. Rhoads, *Manchus and Han* (Seattle: University of Washington Press, 2000).

[7] Kantō Totoku-fu, ed., *Manshū chihō-shi* (Compilation of surveys conducted by Japan's governor-general office in Lüshun) (Kantō Totoku-fu, 1911), vol. 1, 12, 572.

[8] Neiwufu, *Guochao jianye chuji jilüe* (Brief history of the first basis for the foundation of the dynasty) Reprint, 2 vols. (Beijing: Beijing University Press, 1993).

[9] Amagai, *Kōsan*.

[10] Wang Zhonghan, "Guanyu Manzu xingcheng zhong de jige wenti" (Some issues in the formation of the Manchu people) in *Manzu shi yanjiu ji* (Collected works in the study of Manchu history), ed. Wang Zhonghan, (Beijing: Zhongguo shehui kexue chubanshe, 1988), 1–16.

[11] Enatsu Yoshiki, "Shindai no jidai, Tōsanshō ni okeru hakki shōen no sōtō ni tsuite no ichi kōsatsu" (A study of Manchu manor managers in the Three Eastern Provinces during the Qing period), *Shakai Keizaishigaku* 46.1 (1980): 59–76.

[12] James Lee and Cameron Campbell, *Fate and Fortune in Rural China: Social Organization and Population Behavior in Liaoning 1774–1873* (Cambridge: Cambridge University Press, 1997).

[13] Ding Yizhuang, Guo Songyi, Li Zhongqing, and Kang Wenlin, *Liaodong yimin zhong de qiren shehui: Lishi wenxian, renkou tongji yu tianye diaocha* (Banner people society of immigrants in Liaodong: Historical documents, population data, and field surveys), forthcoming.

[14] Ura, "Kangun"; Sudō Yoshiyuki, "Shinchō shoki ni okeru tōjū to sono kigen" (The surrender of Han Chinese to the Manchu and its origin at the beginning of the Qing period) in his *Shindai Higashi Ajia-shi kenkyū* (A study on East Asian history during the Qing period) (Nihon Gakujutsu Shinkōkai, 1972), 1–107;

Amagai, *Naimufu kanshō*; Amagai, *Kōsan*. Wang Zhonghan, Chen Jiahua, and Fu Kedong have also discussed the general features of Han bannermen and their history during the Qing period. See Wang Zhonghan, "Guanyu Manzu xingcheng zhong de jige wenti"; Chen Jiahua and Fu Kedong, "Baqi jianli qian niulu renkou chutan" (A preliminary investigation into Manchurian Niulu and its population before the establishment of the Eight Banner system); Chen Jiahua and Fu Kedong, "Baqi Hanjun gaolüe" (A study of the Han banners), all in Wang Zhonghan's edited volume *Manzu shi yanjiu ji*.

[15] Ura, "Kangun," 818–19

[16] Sudō Yoshiyuki, "Shinchō shoki ni okeru tōjū to sono kigen."

[17] Amagai, *Naimufu kanshō*, 11–21.

[18] Ura, "Kangun," 846–47; Jonathan D. Spence, *Ts'ao Yin and the K'ang-hsi Emperor* (New Haven: Yale University Press, 1965), 7.

[19] Spence, *Ts'ao Yin*, 76.

[20] Ding, Guo, Li, and Kang, *Liaodong yimin zhong de qiren shehui*.

[21] Chen and Fu, "Baqi jianli qian niulu renkou chutan," 280.

[22] Manbun rōtō Kenkyūkai, *Manbun rōtō* (Japanese translation of *Manwen laodang*) (Tōyō Bunko, 1959), vol. 4, 1023–24.

[23] Ura, "Kangun," 818–19.

[24] Sudō, *Shindai Manshū tochi seisaku*, 2–3; Amagai, *Kōsan*, 2–6.

[25] Ding, Guo, Li, and Kang, *Liaodong yimin zhong de qiren shehui*.

[26] Ura, "Kangun" 822–24.

[27] Amagai Kenzaburō, *Suichūken Ryōkaton kanshō shōkachi chōsa hōkoku-sho* (Report of an investigation of former public manor lands in Lingjiatun, Suizhong County) (Tochi Seido Chōsa-kai, 1939), 8, 23.

[28] Oda, *Shinkoku gyōsei-hō*, vol. 2, 22–23, 58–61.

[29] Zhao Erxun et al., eds., *Qingshi gao* (Draft history of the Qing), *juan* 485 (Reprint, Beijing: Zhonghua shuju, 1984), vol. 44, 13, 379.

[30] Spence, *Ts'ao Yin*, 9, 15–16, 23, 157–65, 166–212, 269, 274.

[31] Gugong bowuyuan Ming-Qing dang'anbu, ed., *Guanyu jianing shizao Caojia dang'an shiliao* (Historical materials concerning the Cao family of Jianing Shizao) (Beijing: Zhonghua shuju, 1975).

[32] Spence, *Ts'ao Yin*, 151, 288, 290.

[33] The name of Cao Yin and his career are briefly cited in the descriptions of the *Qingshi gao*.

[34] Spence, *Ts'ao Yin*, 4–5.

[35] Narakino Shimesu, *Shindai jūyō shokkan no kenkyū* (A study on significant posts in the Qing government) (Kazama Shobō, 1975), 60. Kessker has also explained the same point. Lawrence Kessker, *K'ang-hsi and the Consolidation of Ch'ing Rule 1661–1684* (Chicago: University of Chicago Press, 1976), 119–24.

[36] Narakino Shimesu, *Shindai jūyō shokkan no kenkyū*, 61.

[37] Oda, *Shinkoku gyōsei-hō*, vol. 1 (Part 2), 90.

[38] *Fengtian tongzhi* (Local gazetteer of Fengtian), comp. Wang Shunan et al., 1934, *juan* 154.48, 51, 53. (Reprint, Shenyang: Shenyang guji shudian, 1983), vol. 4, 3579, 3581, 3582.

[39] Qian Shifu, *Qingji xinshe zhiguan nianbiao* (Chronological table of new posts in the Qing government) (Beijing: Zhonghua shuju, 1961), 89.

[40] Oda, *Shinkoku gyōsei-hō*, vol. 5, 94–98.

[41] Qin Chengzhi, "Xinhai geming yu Zhang Rong" (The 1911 Revolution and Zhang Rong) in *Xinhai geming huiyilu* (Memoirs of the 1911 Revolution), edited by Zhongguo renmin zhengzhi xieshang huiyi quanguo weiyuanhui wenshi shiliao yanjiu weiyuanhui (Beijing: Zhonghua shudian, 1963), 592–97.

[42] Oda, *Shinkoku gyōsei-hō*, vol. 4, 275.

[43] Narakino, *Shindai jūyō shokkan*, 229; Ura, "Kangun," 836.

[44] Amagai Kenzaburō, *Chūgoku tochi monjo no kenkyū* (Studies on Chinese documents on land) (Keisō Shobō, 1966), 798–99.

[45] *Fengtian tongzhi, juan* 155.74, *juan* 158.18 (vol. 4, 3621, 3668).

[46] Sonoda Kazuki, *Hōtenha no shinjin to kyūjin* (New and old generations of the Fengtian political group) (Fengtian: Manshū Nichi-nichi Shinbunsha, 1922), 91.

[47] *Fengtian tongzhi, juan* 160.49 (vol. 4, 3724).

[48] Yuan Jinkai, *Yulu riji yucun fu jingguo zishu* (Diary of Yulu), vol. 1.15a, deposited at the Liaoning Provincial Library.

[49] The *Qingshi gao* was compiled under the leadership of Zhao Erxun, a Han bannerman, after the fall of the Qing dynasty. Ōtani Takeo, "Shinshikō no seiritsu to sono seikaku" (Compilation of a draft of Qing history and its features) *Mantetsu Chōsa Geppō* 22.9 (1942): 171–82.

[50] *Fengtian tongzhi, juan* 154.22–57; *juan* 156.14–87; *juan* 157.1–37; *juan* 158.1–39 (vol. 4, 3566–84, 3591–627, 3641–79).

Chapter 2

[1] (Manshūkoku) Kokumuin Jitsugyōbu Rinji Sangyō Chōsakyoku, ed. *Kōtoku gannendo nōson jittai chōsa hōkoku-sho kobetu chōsa no bu* (Kōtoku first-year edition: Report of the actual state of agricultural villages, door-to-door inquiry), 3 vols. (Shinkyō, 1935); (Manshūkoku) Kokumuin Jitsugyōbu Rinji Sangyō Chōsakyoku, ed. *Kōtoku 3 nendo nōson jittai chōsa hōkoku-sho kobetu chōsa no bu* (Kōtoku third-year edition: Report of the actual state of agricultural villages, door-to-door inquiry), 4 vols. (Shinkyō, 1936).

[2] Amano Motonosuke, *Manshū keizai no hattatsu* (The development of the Manchurian economy) (Dairen: Minami Manshū Tetsudō Kabushiki Kaisha, 1932), 39–41.

[3] Sonoda, *Hōtenha*, 101.

[4] Qin, "Xinhai geming yu Zhang Rong," 592.

[5] Amano, *Manshū keizai*, 41.

[6] *Fengtian tongzhi, juan* 160.51 (vol. 4, 3725).

[7] Zhou Junshi (trans. by Zheng Ranquan) *Higeki no kōtei Fugi* (Puyi, the tragic emperor) (Kōbunsha, 1984), 186–87.

[8] Li Wenzhi, ed., *Zhongguo jindai nonyeshi ziliao* (Collected sources of agricultural history in modern China) (Beijing: Sanlian shudian, 1957), vol. 1, 194; *Liaoyang xianzhi* (Gazetteer of Liaoyang County), compiled by Fei Huanxing 裴煥星 et al. (Taipei: Chengwen chubanshe, 1973), *juan* 13.4b (vol. 2, 538).

[9] Amagai, *Naimufu kanshō*, 134; Tahara Teijirō, *Shinmatsu Minsho Chūgoku kanshin jinmeiroku* (A directory of Chinese officials at the end of the Qing and the beginning of the Republican periods) (Beijing: Chūgoku kenkyūkai, 1918), 72–73; Amagai, *Chūgoku tochi monjo no kenkyū*, 800; Amagai, *Suichūken Ryōkaton kanshō shōkachi chōsa hōkoku-sho*, 23.

[10] Amagai, *Chūgoku tochi monjo no kenkyū*, 800, 807–14.

[11] Sudō, *Shindai Manshū tochi seisaku*, 2–3, 12. The general structure of the banner land system has also been the subject of recent studies by Chinese scholars. For example, Wang Gesheng examined the general history of the banner lands in Manchuria by consulting a variety of historical documents, such as local gazetteers, *dang'an* materials, and other sources in the *Qingdai Dongbei tudi zhidu shi* (History of the land system in Manchuria during the Qing period) (Shenyang: Liaoning daxue chubanshe, 1991). A valuable compilation of *dang'an* materials is: Zhongguo renmin daxue Qingshi yanjiusuo et al., eds., *Qingdai de qidi* (Banner lands during the Qing period), 3 vols. (Beijing: Zhonghua shuju, 1989); Liaoning sheng dang'anguan, ed., *Shengjing Neiwufu liangzhuang dang'an huibian* (Collected *dang'an* materials about manors of Shengjing Neiwufu), 2 vols. (Shenyang: Liaoshen shushe, 1993).

[12] Amagai, *Suichūken Ryōkaton kanshō shōkachi chōsa hōkoku-sho*, 8.

[13] Amagai, *Kōsan*, 1.

[14] Manshūkoku Tochikyoku, *Manshū ni okeru tochi seido no gaiyō* (An overview of the land system in Manchuria) (Shinkyō, 1935), 42–53.

[15] Sudō, "Shinchō shoki ni okeru tōjū."

[16] Amagai, *Naimufu kanshō*, 11–21, 141–72. Muramatsu Yūji also examined a document concerning an unidentified Manchu noble's manor land in southern Manchuria during the Qing period. Inquiring into this particular document, Muramatsu noted the existence of a Han Chinese style of landlord-tenant relationship existing within the framework of the Manchu manor system. Muramatsu Yūji, "Kenryū jidai kakyū Manshū kizoku no chisan to jintei" (Lands and peasants of the lower Manchu nobles during the Qianlong period), *Tōyōshi Kenkyū* 28.4 (1970): 75–98.

[17] Arthur W. Hummel, *Eminent Chinese of the Ch'ing Period* (*1644–1912*) (Washington, D.C.: United States Government Printing Office, 1944), vol. 2, 672–73. Sun Jiagan was appointed *xieban daxueshi* (assistant grand secretary) and *libu shangshu* (minister of the Personnel Ministry) during the time of the Qianlong reign (1736–1795).

[18] Sun Jiagan, "Baqi gongchan shu" (Memorials regarding the Eight Banner lands) in *Huangchao jingshi wenbian, juan* 35.10b–11a. Reprinted in *Jindai Zhongguo shiliao congkan*, sec. 74 (Historical sources on modern China) (Taipei: Wenhai chubanshe, 1964), vol. 3, 1278–80.

[19] Zhang Tingxiang was a *jinshi* from Zhili. See Zhu Baojiong and Xie Peilin, eds., *Ming-Qing jinshi timing beilu suoyin* (An index of *jinshi* names in the Ming-Qing periods) (Shanghai: Shanghai guji chubanshe, 1963), 421.

[20] Zhongguo kexueyuan Jili sheng fenyuan lishi yanjiusuo, Jilin shifan daxue lishixi, ed., *Jindai Dongbei renmin geming yundong shi* (Revolutionary movements in the modern Northeast provinces) (Changchun: Jilin renmin chubanshe, 1960), 11.

[21] Amagai, *Chūgoku tochi monjyo no kenkyū*, 807–14.

[22] Oda, *Shinkoku gyōsei-hō*, vol. 1 (Part 2), 94–98.

[23] I examined the disposition of official land in Fengtian in the following articles. Enatsu Yoshiki, "Shinmatsu no jiki, Tōsanshō nanbu ni okeru kanchi no jōhō no shakai keizaishi teki imi" (The social-economic significance of the disposition of official land in southern Dongsansheng at the end of the Qing dynasty), *Shakai Keizaishigaku* 49.4 (1983): 28–47; Enatsu Yoshiki, "Shingai kakumei go, kyū Hōtenshō ni okeru kanyūchi no haraisage ni tsuite" (The disposition of official land in Fengtian Province after the 1911 Revolution), *Hitotsubashi Ronsō* 98.6 (1987): 23–42.

[24] Zhongguo kexueyuan lishi yanjiusuo disan suo, ed., *Xiliang weigao caogao* (Collected works of Xiliang), *juan* 7, document no. 1131. (Reprint, Beijing: Zhonghua shudian, 1959), vol. 2, 1248–51.

[25] *Xiliang weigao caogao, juan* 7, document no. 1021 (vol. 2, 1117).

[26] Xu Shichang, *Dongsansheng zhenglüe* (The administration of the Three Eastern Provinces), *juan* 7.3a–5b. (Reprint, Taipei: Chengwen chubanshe, 1965), vol. 9, 5021–26.

[27] *Dongsansheng zhenglüe, juan* 7.14a (vol. 9, 5043).

[28] Fengtian nongshi shiyanchang, ed., *Fengtian quansheng nongye diaocha shu, di 1 qi* (Report of an investigation of agriculture in Fengtian Province, Part 1) (Fengtian, 1909), vol. 5-2.40a.

[29] Amagai, *Suichūken Ryōkaton kanshō shōkachi chōsa hōkoku-sho*, 8.

[30] The average acreage of land cultivated by household in Guangning and Yizhou in the Jinzhou area was 20–30 *mu* at the end of the Qing period. *Fengtian quansheng nongye diaocha shu, di 1 qi*, vol. 5-2.46b–47a.

[31] *Xiliang weigao caogao, juan* 7, document no. 910 (vol. 2, 975–76).

[32] *Xiliang weigao caogao, juan* 7, document no. 1021 (vol. 2, 1117).

[33] Xu Shichang, *Dongsansheng zhenglüe, juan* 7.9a (vol. 9, 5033).

[34] Amagai, *Chūgoku tochi monjo no kenkyū*, 809–10, 814.

[35] Amagai, *Naimufu kanshō*, 36, 109–110.

[36] *Xiliang weigao caogao, juan* 7, document no. 910 (vol. 2, 975–76).

[37] Ibid.

[38] Amagai, *Suichūken Ryōkaton kanshō shōkachi chōsa hōkoku-sho,* 8.

[39] *Suichūken Ryōkaton kanshō shōkachi chōsa hōkoku-sho*, 6, 24. For example, in Dashicaotun of Suizhong County, some tenant-peasants of the Jinzhou manors were allowed to buy all the manor land in their village. (Manshūkoku) Kokumuin Sangyōbu Nōmushi ed., *Kōtoku 4 nendo Kengishi minaraisei nōson jittai chōsa hōkoku-sho, Kinshū-shō Suichū-ken* (Kōtoku fourth-year edition, Report of the actual state of the agricultural villages by officials in training, Suizhong County, Jinzhou Province) (Shinkyō, 1938), 232–41.

[40] Xu Shichang, *Tuigengtang congshu* (Collected works of Tuigengtang), *juan* 20, 27a–28b. Reprinted in *Jindai zhonguo shiliao congkan, di 23 ji*, edited by Shen Yunlong et al. (Taipei: Wenhai chubanshe, 1964).

[41] Amagai, *Suichūken Ryōkaton kanshō shōkachi chōsa hōkoku-sho*, 14, 39–42.

[42] Qin, "Xinhai geming yu Zhang Rong," 592.

[43] Amagai, *Kōsan*, 262–85.

[44] I examine the incident that involved the attempted sale of Zhaoling yaochai guandiandi in the article "Shingai kakumei go kyū Hōten-shō ni okeru kanchi no haraisage"(The disposition of official land in Fengtian after the 1911 Revolution), *Tōyōshi Kenkyū* 53.3 (1994): 103–27.

Chapter 3

[1] Oda, *Shinkoku gyōsei-hō*, vol. 1 (Part 2), 262–67.

[2] Sonoda, *Hōtenha*, 6.

[3] Oda, *Shinkoku gyōsei-hō*, vol. 3, 393–95.

[4] Chang P'eng-yüan, *Lixian pai yu Xinhai geming* (Constitutionalists and the 1911 Revolution) (Taipei: Zhongguo xueshu zhuzuo jiangzhu weiyuanhui, 1969), 1–4.

[5] Oda, *Shinkoku gyōsei-hō*, vol. 1 (Part 2), 94–98.

[6] *Fengtian tongzhi, juan* 135.47 (vol. 3, 3080).

[7] Xu Shichang, *Dongsansheng zhenglüe, juan* 6 (vol. 7, 3647–4328).

[8] Oda, *Shinkoku gyōsei-hō*, vol. 1 (Part 2), 95; *Fengtian tongzhi, juan* 135.47–53 (vol. 3, 3080–83).

[9] Oda, *Shinkoku gyōsei-hō*, vol. 1 (Part 2), 97–98; *Fengtian tongzhi, juan* 135.53–62 (vol. 3, 3083–87).

[10] Masubuchi Tatsuo, "Rekishi ninshiki ni okeru shōko shugi to genjitsu hihan" (Classicism and critique of reality in the understanding of history) in *Rekishi-ka no dōjidai-shi teki kōsatsu ni tsuite* (Historians' investigation into contemporary history), by Masubuchi Tatsuo (Iwanami Shoten, 1983), 171–224.

[11] Oda, *Shinkoku gyōsei-hō*, vol. 1 (Part 2), 236–38.

[12] *Fengtian tongzhi, juan* 141.46 (vol. 3, 3246).

[13] *Fengtian tongzhi, juan* 141.51 (vol. 3, 3248); Gaimushō Jōhō-bu, *Gendai Shina jinmeikan* (A directory of contemporary Chinese) (Tokyo, 1924), 168–69.

[14] *Fengtian tongzhi, juan* 141.51–52 (vol. 3, 3248–49).

[15] Gaimushō, *Gendai Shina jinmeikan*, 833.

[16] *Fengtian tongzhi, juan* 135.22, 36, 40; *juan* 141.53, 62–63, (vol. 3, 3067, 3074, 3076, 3249, 3254).

[17] *Fengtian tongzhi, juan* 141.49–50 (vol. 3, 3247–48); Gaimushō, *Gendai Shina jinmeikan*, 728–29.

[18] Shi Jichang held the office of director general of Political Affairs in the Fengtian provincial government in 1915 and 1918. Tan Guohuan was appointed director general of Business Affairs and secretary general to the Chief Commander of the Dongsansheng office in the Zhang Zuolin government. See Sonoda, *Hōtenha*, 80–86, 103–9.

[19] Rong Hou held such offices as director of Foreign Affairs in Yingkou, president of the Central Bank of Manchuria, and so forth, under the Zhang Zuolin and Manzhouguo governments. Gaimushō Jōhō-bu, ed., *Gendai Chūka Minkoku Manshū teikoku jinmeikan, Shōwa 12 nen ban* (A directory of important people in contemporary Republic of China and Manzhouguo, 1937 edition) (Tōa dōbunkai, 1937), 617.

[20] Chang P'eng-yüan, *Lixian pai yu Xinhai geming*, 26–32.

[21] Kantō Totoku-fu, ed., *Manshū ippan-shi sōkō* (General history of Manchuria, manuscript) (Kantō Totoku-fu, 1911), 445–79.

[22] Chang P'eng-yüan, *Lixian pai yu Xinhai geming*, 63–104.

[23] Li Shou-k'ung, "Gesheng ziyiju lianhehui yu Xinhai geming" (Association of Provincial Assemblies and the 1911 Revolution) in *Zhongguo xiandai shi congkan, di 3 ce* (Studies on the history of contemporary China) (Taipei: Zhengzhong shuju, 1962), vol. 3, 353–54.

[24] Xu Shichang, *Dongsansheng zhenglüe, juan* 6.23 (vol. 7, 3707).

[25] Ibid.

[26] *Dongsansheng zhenglüe, juan* 6.16 (vol. 7, 3693–94).

[27] *Dongsansheng zhenglüe, juan* 6.23 (vol. 7, 3707).

[28] *Dongsansheng zhenglüe, juan* 6.35 (vol. 7, 3731).

[29] *Dongsansheng zhenglüe, juan* 6.34 (vol. 7, 3729).

[30] *Xiliang yigao caogao, juan* 7, document nos. 1021, 1161 (vol. 2, 1117, 1278).

[31] He Donglin, "Xinhai geming zai Liaoyang" (The 1911 Revolution in Liaoyang) in *Xinhai geming huiyilu* (Memoirs of the 1911 Revolution), vol. 5, 566.

[32] Joseph W. Esherick, *Reform and Revolution in China* (Berkley: University of California Press, 1975), 93

[33] Xu Shichang, *Dongsansheng zhenglüe, juan* 6.17a–21b (vol. 7, 3695–3704).

[34] *Fengtian tongzhi, juan* 160.49 (vol. 4, 3724).

[35] Tanabe Tanejirō, *Tōsanshō kanshin-roku* (A Directory of officials in the Three Eastern Provinces) (Dairen: Tōsanshō Kanshin-roku Kankōkai, 1924), 833.

[36] *Tōsanshō kanshin-roku*, 96.

[37] *Tōsanshō kanshin-roku*, 340.

[38] *Tōsanshō kanshin-roku*, 343.

[39] *Tōsanshō kanshin-roku*, 352.

[40] *Tōsanshō kanshin-roku*, 187.

[41] *Hailong xianzhi* (Local gazetteer of Hailong County), comp. Bai Yongzhen et al., 1913, *juan* 4.21b–24b; He Donglin, "Xinhai geming zai Liaoyang," 566.

[42] Xu Shichang, *Dongsansheng zhenglüe, juan* 6.25–26 (vol. 7, 3712–13).

[43] *Dongsansheng zhenglüe, juan* 6.46–47 (vol. 7, 3753–56).

[44] Starting with the general population of eligible voters, the preparatory elections narrowed the field to a sort of electoral college, which then selected the final candidates from among its own number.

[45] *Xiliang yigao caogao, juan* 7, document no. 899 (vol. 2, 965).

[46] Chang P'eng-yüan, *Lixian pai yu Xinhai geming*, 13–14.

[47] The average land price was about 27 *yuan* per *mu* in Liaoyang, quite a high price, and 10–16 *yuan* per *mu* in other remote areas. *Fengtian quansheng nongye diaocha shu, di 1 qi*, vol. 5-2.39a–41b.

[48] *Fengtian quansheng nongye diaocha shu*, 5-2.46b–47a.

[49] Zhang Huanyu was also elected as a member of the Provincial Assembly (*shengyihui*) after the 1911 Revolution. *Fengtian tongzhi, juan* 160.52–53 (vol. 4, 3725–26). As an influential member of the Zhang family, he was appointed manager of Datong Bank, which was founded by Zhang Huanxiang and Ding Chao in Fushun in 1922. Fujii Ryō, *Manshu ni okeru shina ginkō no gaiyō* (An outline of Chinese banks in Manchuria) (Dairen: Minami Manshū Tetsudō Kabushiki Kaisha, 1929), 41. Gaimushō, *Gendai Shina jinmeikan*, 400.

[50] Esherick, *Reform and Revolution in China*, 100.

[51] Sonoda, *Hōtenha*, 91; *Fengtian tongzhi, juan* 160.2 (vol. 4, 3700).

[52] *Fengtian tongzhi, juan* 160.18 (vol. 4, 3708).

[53] Chang P'eng-yüan, *Lixian pai yu Xinhai geming*, 248.

[54] *Fengtian tongzhi, juan* 155.74; *juan* 157.10; *juan* 158.18 (vol. 4, 3621, 3645, 3668).

[55] *Xiliang yigao caogao, juan* 7, document no. 1109 (vol. 2, 1219).

Chapter 4

[1] Sonoda, *Hōtenha,* 84.

[2] Gaimushō, *Gendai Chūka Minkoku,* 433.

[3] Yuan Qingxuan, "Yuan Jinkai nianpu" (Chronological record of Yuan Jinkai) in *Liaoyang wenshi ziliao* (Historical documents of Liaoyang) (Liaoyang: Liaoyang wenshi ziliao chubanshe, 1992), vol. 6, 151–61; Zhi Xin and Gui Dong, "Yuan Jinkai de yisheng"(The life of Yuan Jinkai) in *Liaoyang wenshi ziliao*, vol. 7, 166–96; Yamaguchi Shigetsugu, *Kieta teikoku Manshū* (Manzhouguo, the empire that disappeared) (Mainichi Shinbunsha, 1967), 246.

[4] Sonoda. *Hōtenha,* 84.

[5] Tamura Jitsuzō, *Chūgoku seifuku ōchō no kenkyū* (Studies of conqueror dynasties in China) (Kyoto; Tōyōshi Kenkyūkai, 1964), vol. 1, 327.

[6] Oshino Akio, "Ryōyō" (Liaoyang) in *Ajia rekishi jiten* (Encyclopedia of Asian history) (Heibonsha, 1960), vol. 9, 308.

[7] Gaimushō, *Gendai Chūka Minkoku,* 616, 655, 692, 638.

[8] Dazai Matsusaburō, *Manshū gendai shi* (A contemporary history of Manchuria) (Dairen: Minami Manshū Tetsudō Kabushiki Kaisha, 1923), 224.

[9] Li Wenzhi, ed., *Zhongguo jindai nonyeshi shiliao* (Collected sources of agricultural history in modern China) (Beijing: Sanlian shudian, 1957), vol. 1, 194; *Liaoyang xianzhi, juan* 13.4b (vol. 2, 538).

[10] Zhou, *Higeki no kōtei Fugi*, 186–87.

[11] Amagai, *Naimufu kanshō*, 62–64; Oda, *Shinkoku gyōsei-hō*, vol. 4, 278.

[12] Chao Chung-fu, "Qingdai Dongsansheng gufei wenti zhi tantao" (Frontier outlaws in Manchuria, 1890–1930) in *Zhongyang yanjiuyuan hindaishi yanjiusuo qikan, di 7 qi* (1978): 509–25.

[13] Sonoda, *Hōtenha*, 5.

[14] Sonoda, *Hōtenha*, 94.

[15] Yoshida Kin'ichi, "Ba Senzan" (Ma Zhanshan) in *Ajia rekishi jiten*, vol. 7, 374.

[16] Wada Kiyoshi, *Chūgoku chihō jichi hattatsu-shi [Eiin-ban]* (History of the development of self-government in China, reprint edition) (Kyūko Shoin, 1975), 169–74.

[17] See for instance, Philip Kuhn, *Rebellion and Its Enemies in Late Imperial China* (Cambridge, Mass.: Harvard University Press, 1970), 102–3.

[18] *Liaoyang xianzhi, juan* 22.9a–12b (vol. 3, 859–66).

[19] *Liaoyang xianzhi, juan* 22.9a (vol. 3. 859–60).

[20] *Liaoyang xianzhi, juan* 21.8b (vol. 3, 836).

[21] Ibid.

[22] *Liaoyang xianzhi, juan* 22.9b (vol. 3, 860).

[23] *Fengtian tongzhi, juan* 160.51 (vol. 4, 3725); Sanbō Honbu, *Meiji 37, 38 nen Nichiro sensō-shi* (History of the Russo-Japanese War, 1904–1905) (Tōkyō Kaikōsha, 1912), vol. 3, 175.

[24] *Liaoyang xianzhi, juan* 22.10b (vol. 3, 862).

[25] *Liaoyang xianzhi, juan* 22.12a (vol. 3, 865).

[26] *Liaoyang xianzhi, juan* 22.10a (vol. 3, 861).

[27] *Liaoyang xianzhi, juan* 22.11a (vol. 3, 863).

[28] *Liaoyang xianzhi, juan* 22.7a (vol. 3, 855).

[29] *Jindai Dongbei renmin geming yundong shi*, 172, 178–79, 222–23.

[30] Feng Shaotang was a Qing bureaucrat and was appointed staff member of the Hanlin Academy. After the Russo-Japanese War, the Qing government sent him to Japan to study government institutions. At the time of the Boxer Rebellion, Feng Shaotang returned from Beijing to his native Liaoyang. He petitioned the Shengjing military governor, Zeng Qi, to allow him to form a local militia, along with powerful Liaoyang figures such as Liu Chunlang and De Bin, and the local elite in neighboring counties such as Haicheng, Xinmin, and Guangning. He also recommended that Feng Lin'ge, his nephew, be appointed commander of the local militia in the border area between Liaoyang and Haicheng counties. At that time Feng Lin'ge was a leader of the bandits (*lulin*) in Liaoyang. In other words, Feng Shaotang tried to defend villages of this area from bandit invasions by using bandit forces as the basis of the local militia. *Liaoyang xianzhi, juan* 9.26a–26b (vol. 2, 441–42), *juan* 21.9a (vol. 3, 837).

[31] *Liaoyang xianzhi, juan* 9.26a (vol. 2, 441).

[32] *Liaoyang xianzhi, juan* 9.22b–23a (vol. 2, 434–35).

[33] Qin, "Xinhai geming yu Zhang Rong," 595–97.

[34] *Jindai Dongbei renmin geming yundong shi*, 172, 178–79, 222–23.

[35] Elizabeth Perry, *Rebels and Revolutionaries in North China* (Stanford: Stanford University Press, 1980).

[36] Kuhn, *Rebellion and Its Enemies*, 165–75.

[37] *Liaoyang xianzhi, juan* 22.6b (vol. 3, 854.

[38] *Dongsansheng zhenglüe, juan* 6.67a–68a (vol. 7, 3795–97).

[39] *Xiliang yigao caogao, juan* 7, document no. 899 (vol. 2, 963).

[40] *Xiliang yigao caogao, juan* 7, document no. 1021 (vol. 2, 1116).

[41] *Xiliang yigao caogao, juan* 7, document no. 1161 (vol. 2, 1278).

[42] Kuhn, *Rebellion and Its Enemies*, 67, 93–97.

[43] *Liaoyang xianzhi, juan* 22.6b (vol. 3, 854).

[44] *Xiliang yigao caogao, juan* 7, document no. 1021 (vol. 2, 1116).

[45] *Dongsansheng zhenglüe, juan* 6.86a (vol. 7, 3833); *Fengtian tongzhi, juan* 143.1 (vol. 3, 3264).

[46] *Fengtian tongzhi, juan* 143.6 (vol. 3, 3267).

[47] *Dongsansheng zhenglüe, juan* 6.92a, 96a (vol. 7, 3845, 3853).

[48] *Dongsansheng zhenglüe, juan* 6.92a (vol. 7, 3845).

[49] *Dongsansheng zhenglüe, juan* 6.94a (vol. 7, 3849); *Fengtian tongzhi, juan* 143.4 (vol. 3, 3266).

[50] *Dongsansheng zhenglüe, juan* 6.67b (vol. 7, 3796).

[51] Sonoda, *Hōtenha*, 55, 84.

[52] He, "Xinhai geming zai Liaoyang," 596.

[53] (Manshūkoku) Kokumuin tōkei Hensan-sho, ed., *Dai 1 ji Manshūkoku nenpō* (First annual report of Manzhouguo) (Shinkyō: Kokumuin Tōkei-sho, 1933), 11–13.

[54] *Xiliang yigao caogao, juan* 7, document no. 899 (vol. 2, 965).

[55] *Fengtian tongzhi, juan* 160.51 (vol. 4, 3725).

[56] *Xiliang weigao caogao, juan* 7, document no. 1021 (vol. 2, 1115).

[57] *Xiliang yigao caogao, juan* 7, document no. 1109 (vol. 2, 1219).

[58] Kantō Totoku-fu, *Manshū ippan-shi sōkō dai 2 satsu*, 1219.

[59] *Liaoyang xianzhi, juan* 23.1b–8b, (vol. 3, 868–82).

[60] Esherick, *Reform and Revolution in China*, 110–11.

Chapter 5

[1] Nishimura Shigeo, "Tōsanshō ni okeru Shingai Kakumei" (The 1911 Revolution in Manchuria), ***Rekishigaku kenkyū*** 358 (1970): 25.

[2] Li Shiyue, "Xinhai geming shiqi, Dongsansheng geming yu fan geming de douzheng" (The struggle between revolutionaries and anti-revolutionaries in Dongsansheng at the time of the 1911 Revolution), *Lishi yanjiu* 1959.6 (1959): 62–63; Nishimura, "Tōsanshō," 18.

[3] Zhang Xia, Sun Baoming, and Chen Zhanghe, eds., *Beiyang lujun shiliao, 1912–1916* (Historical sources of Beiyang Army, 1912–1916) (Tianjin: Tianjin renmin chubanshe, 1982), 117, 139.

[4] Ning Wu, "Dongbei Xinhai geming jianshu" (A brief summary of the 1911 Revolution in Manchuria) in *Xinhai geming huiyilu*, vol. 5, 536.

[5] Oda, *Shinkoku gyōsei-hō*, vol. 4, 369–70.

[6] *Jindai Dongbei shi*, 375; Li, "Xinhai geming shiqi," 63; *Jindai Dongbei renmin yundong shi*, 215.

[7] *Jindai Dongbei shi*, 376.

[8] Nishimura, "Tōsanshō," 19, 21.

[9] *Jindai Dongbei shi*, 373.

[10] *Jindai Dongbei shi*, 372; Li, "Xinhai geming shiqi," 62; *Jindai Dongbei renmin yundong shi*, 208.

[11] *Jindai Dongbei renmin yundongshi*, 221–22; *Jindai Dongbei shi*, 382–83

[12] Ning, "Dongbei Xinhai," 536.

[13] Li, "Xinhai geming shiqi," 64

[14] *Jindai Dongbei shi*, 374.

[15] *Jindai Dongbei shi*, 375.

[16] *Jindai Dongbei shi*, 374; Li, "Xinhai geming shiqi," 64.

[17] Nishimura, "Tōsanshō," 20; *Jindai Dongbei renmin yundong shi*, 233.

[18] *Shengjing shibao*, 24th day of the ninth month in Xuantong 3.

[19] *Jindai Dongbei renmin yundong shi*, 216.

[20] *Jindai Dongbei shi*, 376; *Jindai Dongbei renmin yundong shi*, 213–14.

[21] *Jindai Dongbei shi*, 377; *Jindai Dongbei renmin yundong shi*, 214.

[22] *Jindai Dongbei shi*, 378; *Jindai Dongbei renmin yundong shi*, 218.

[23] *Jindai Dongbei renmin yundong shi*, 218; Qin, "Xinhai geming yu Zhang Rong," 601.

[24] *Jindai Dongbei renmin yundong shi*, 219.

[25] *Jindai Dongbei shi*, 379.

[26] *Jindai Dongbei shi*, 381–83; Li,"Xinhai geming shiqi," 65–66; *Jindai Dongbei renmin yundong shi*, 221–23.

[27] Qin, "Xinhai geming yu Zhang Rong," 603–4; *Jindai Dongbei shi*, 389; *Jindai Dongbei renmin yundong shi*, 232. Also, the Chinese archival journal *Lishi Dang'an* includes a report from Zhang Zuolin to Zhao Erxun detailing the actual assassination of Zhang Rong. In reply to Zhang Zuolin's report, Zhao Erxun praised Zhang Zuolin's meritorious deeds and called Zhang Rong a bandit (see *Lishi dang'an* 1981.4 [1981]: 22–23). Zhang Gui, Zhang Rong's elder sister, who escaped from Fengtian immediately after Rong's assassination, reported his case to Sun Wen, and a memorial ceremony is said to have been held for Zhang Rong in Nanjing. After the establishment of the Republic, Zhang Gui reported the details of Zhang Rong's assassination before the House of the Representatives in Beijing, thanks to the arrangements made by Wu Jinglian, who had assumed the position of Speaker of the House. At the same time, Zhang Gui tried to sue Zhao Erxun, Zhang Zuolin, and Yuan Jinkai in the Supreme Court in Beijing for assassinating Zhang Rong, but her attempt failed due to Yuan Shikai's interference in the case; see Qin, "Xinhai geming yu Zhang Rong," 607.

[28] *Jindai Dongbei shi*, 390–91; *Jindai Dongbei renmin yundong shi*, 235–39; Li Shiyue, "Xinhai geming," 68–69.

[29] *Jindai Dongbei renmin yundong shi*, 239–40; Li, "Xinhai geming," 69.

[30] *Jindai Dongbei shi*, 376; *Jindai Dongbei renmin yundong shi*, 213–14.

[31] Zhongguo diyi lishi dang'anguan, ed., *Qingdai dang'an shiliao congpian, di 8 ji, Dongsansheng Xinhai geming shiliao* (Collection of *dang'an* materials in the Qing

period, vol. 8: Historical materials of the 1911 Revolution in Manchuria) (Beijing: Zhonghua shudian, 1982), 15 (document no. 31).

[32] Ibid.

[33] *Qingdai dang'an shiliao congpian*, vol. 8, 16.

[34] *Qingdai dang'an shiliao congpian,* vol. 8, 15.

[35] *Qingdai dang'an shiliao congpian,* vol. 8, 14 (document no. 29).

[36] *Shengjing shibao*, 24th day of the ninth month in Xuantong 3.

[37] *Shengjing shibao*, 27th day of the ninth month in Xuantong 3.

[38] *Qingdai dang'an shiliao congpian*, vol. 8, 16 (document no. 31).

[39] *Qingdai dang'an shiliao congpian,* vol. 8. Two other important works on this event are: Liaoning sheng dang'anguan, ed., *Xinhai geming zai Liaoning dang'an shiliao* (Archival materials concerning the 1911 Revolution in Liaoning) (Shenyang: Liaoning sheng dang'anguan, 1981); Shenyangshi dang'anguan, ed., *Xinhai geming zai Shenyang* (The 1911 Revolution in Shenyang) (Shenyang: Shenyang chubanshe, 1991).

[40] Enatsu Yoshiki, "Chūgoku tōhoku chiiki-shi kenkyū to tōan shiryō," (A study of the local history and archives of Northeastern China with reference to local administration and land affairs) Tōyōshi Kenkyū 58.3 (1999): 173–93.

[41] *Qingdai dang'an shiliao congpian*, vol. 8, 40–41 (document no. 68).

[42] *Qingdai dang'an shiliao congpian,* vol. 8, 126 (document no. 211).

[43] *Qingdai dang'an shiliao congpian,* vol. 8, 217 (document nos. 212 and 213).

[44] *Qingdai dang'an shiliao congpian,* vol. 8, 110–11 (document no. 173).

[45] Qin, "Xinhai geming yu Zhang Rong," 596.

[46] *Qingdai dang'an shiliao congpian,* vol. 8, 110 (document no. 172).

[47] *Qingdai dang'an shiliao congpian,* vol. 8, 167 (document no. 298).

[48] *Qingdai dang'an shiliao congpian,* vol. 8, 91–92 (document no. 151).

[49] Pekin Shina Kenkyūkai, ed., *Saishin Shina kanshin-roku* (The latest directory of Chinese officials) (Beijing: Shina Kenkyūkai, 1918), 150.

[50] Gaimushō, *Gendai Chūka Minkoku,* 654.

[51] Qin, "Xinhai geming yu Zhang Rong," 593, 602.

[52] *Qingdai dang'an shiliao congpian*, vol, 8, 132–33, 136–37, 142–43 (document nos. 225, 231, and 241).

[53] *Qingdai dang'an shiliao congpian,* vol. 8, 132–33 (document no. 225).

[54] *Qingdai dang'an shiliao congpian,* vol. 8, 136–37 (document no. 231).

[55] Ibid.

[56] Esherick, *Reform and Revolution*; Mary Rankin, *Elite Acitivism and Political Transformation in China* (Stanford: Stanford University Press, 1986).

[57] *Qingdai dang'an shiliao congpian*, vol. 8, 208 (document no. 353).

Conclusion

[1] Katō Shigeshi, "Kandai ni okeru kokka zaisei to teishitsu zaisei tono kubetsu narabini teishitsu zaisei ippan" (Distinction between government finances and Imperial Household finances and a general explanation about Imperial Household finances) in Katō Shigeshi, *Shina keizaishi kōshō* (A study of Chinese economic history) (Tōyō Bunko, 1953).

[2] Gaimushō, *Gendai Chūka Minkoku*, 433.

[3] Ibid.

[4] Ibid.

[5] Sonoda, *Hōtenha*, 85.

[6] Gaimushō, *Gendai Chūka Minkoku*, 433.

[7] Ibid.

[8] Ukon, "Manshū tōchi to jinushi kaikyū," (The governing of Manchuria and the landlord class), *Manshū Hyōron* 8.2 (1935): 2–3. Ukon is believed to be the pen name of the journalist Tachibana Shiraki.

[9] Gaimushō, *Gendai Chūka Minkoku*, 433.

Glossary

An Lushan 安禄山

baoanhui 保安会
baojia 保甲
baoyi 包衣
baqi 八旗
Baqi Hanjun 八旗漢軍
Beiling 北陵
benji huibi 本籍廻避
bingyin 丙寅

canyifu canyi 参議府参議
Cao Xueqin 曹雪芹
Cao Yin 曹寅
Chen Zhaochang 陳昭常

Da Zhong gongbao 大中公報
daidi touchong 带地投充
dang'an 档案
Diaochayuan yangchenghui 調査員養成会
difang weichi weiyuanhui 地方維持委員会
Ding Xiaoshu 鄭孝胥
dishi caizheng 帝室財政
Dongbei baoan weiyuanhui 東北保安委員会
Dongbeibu 東北部
Dongjing Liaoyangfu 東京遼陽府
Dongling 東陵
Dongsansheng 東三省
dongshihui 董事会
dubu tang 督部堂
dudu 都督

ejen 額真
engong 恩貢

fen 分
Feng Delin 馮徳麟
Feng Guifen 馮桂芬
Feng Lin'ge 馮麟閣
Feng Shaotang 馮紹唐
fengjian 封建
Fengren zhi Feng 奉人治奉
Fengtian 奉天
Fengtian difang weichi weiyuanhui 奉天地方維持委員会
Fengtian difang zizhihui 奉天地方自治会
Fengtian nongshi shiyanchang 奉天農事試験場
Fengtian sheng gongshu 奉天省公署
fu 府
fubu yuan 撫部院
Fuling 福陵

Gao Qinghe 高清和
gaodeng xunjing xuetang 高等巡警学堂
Geng Zhongming 耿仲明
gengzi 庚子
gongbu 工部
gongsheng 貢生
gongbu shangshu 工部尚書
Gu Renbang 顧仁邦
Gu Renyi 顧仁宜
Gu Yanwu 顧炎武
guandi 官地
Guandi qingzhangju 官地清丈局
guanwai dudu 関外都督
guanzhuang qiding 官荘旗丁
gufei 股匪
guojia caizheng 国家財政
gusa 固山

Hanjun 漢軍
Hanjun qiren 漢軍旗人
Hanren 漢人
Heilongjiang 黒龍江
honghuzi 紅胡子
Honglou meng 紅楼夢
hongyi pao 紅夷砲
Hou Jin 後金
Huang Xing 黄興
hubu 戸部
hufei 胡匪
hukouce 戸口冊

Inukai Tsuyoshi 犬養毅

jiachen 甲辰
jiawu 甲午
jiangjun 将軍
Jian Wenxian 姜文憲
jiao 角
jiapu 家譜
Jilin 吉林
Jingshi daxuetang 京師大学堂
jinshi 進士
jingwuzhang 警務長
junxian 郡縣
juren 举人

Kang Youwei 康有為
Kantō-chō 関東庁
Kantō-gun 関東軍
Kantō-shū 関東州
Kantō Totoku-fu 関東都督府
kenwu dachen 墾務大臣
Kenwuju 墾務局
Kodera Sōkichi 小寺壮吉

Lan Tianyu 藍天蔚
Li Dehu 李徳瑚
Li Lianying 李蓮英
libu 吏部
liang 両
liangchan 糧桟
Lianhe jijinhui 聯合急進会
lianzhuanghui 聯荘会
Liaoning 遼寧
Liaoyang donglu xunjing shiwu 遼陽東路巡警事務
Liaoyang xilu xunjing shiwu 遼陽西路巡警事務
Liaoyang zizhi qichenghui 遼陽自治期成会
Ling Yunge 凌雲閣

linsheng 廩生
Liu Danian 柳大年
Liu Donglang 劉東烺
Liu Enge 劉恩閣
longmo 龍脈
longqi 龍気
lulin 緑林
Luo Zhenyu 羅振玉

Ma Zhanshan 馬占山
Manshū Hyōron 滿洲評論
Mantetsu 滿鉄
Manwen laodang 滿文老档
Manzhou fengjin 滿洲封禁
Manzhouguo 滿洲国
Manzhou zhaomin kaikenli 滿洲招民開墾例
mazei 馬賊
minjie 民界
minren 民人
min yamen 民衙門
Minami Manshū Tetsudō Kabushiki Kaisha 南滿洲鉄道株式会社
minzhengshi 民政使
minzu 民族
Mou Weixin 牟維新
mu 畝

Neiwufu 内務府
niru 牛彔
Nishimiya Fusajirō 西宮房次郎

Puyi 溥儀

qi yamen 旗衙門
qian 銭
qianshi 僉事
qianwei beidi 前衛北地
qidi 旗地
qingli caizheng guanliguan 清理財政管理官
qijie 旗界
Qin Zhifan 秦之藩
qiren 旗人
Qiwusi 旗務司
Quan Tangshi 全唐詩
Quansheng zizhiju 全省自治局

ri 日
Rong Hou 栄厚

Sanling 三陵
shang 晌
shangshu 尚書
Shang Kexi 尚可喜
shangsanqi 上三旗
shangshufu dachen 尚書府大臣
shaoguo 焼鍋
Shengjing 盛京
Shengjing libu 盛京礼部
Shengjing shibao 盛京時報
shengyihui 省議会
shengyuan 生員
Shi Jichang 史紀常
Shi Siming 史思明
Shuihu zhuan 水滸伝
Song Jiaoren 宋教仁
suigong 歳貢
Sun Jiagan 孫嘉淦
Sun Qichang 孫其昌
Sun Xiaozong 孫孝宗
Tan Guangqing 談広慶

Tan Guohuan 談国桓
Tian Yugong 田雨公
tidiao 題調
ting 庁
Ting Mao 廷茂
Tochikyoku 土地局
Tongmenghui 同盟会
tuanfang 团防
tuanlian 团練
Tunkenju 屯墾局

Wang Chengxian 王成憲
Wang Shaozhen 王少臣
Wang Yintang 王蔭棠
Wang Yuquan 王玉泉
Wenshi ziliao 文史資料
Wu Enpei 呉恩培
Wu Jinglian 呉景廉
Wu Sangui 呉三桂
Wu Yue 呉樾

xian 縣
xiangbai 鑲白
xianghong 鑲紅
xianghuang 鑲黄
xianglan 鑲藍
xiangtuan 郷团
Xie Shulin 謝書林
Xiliang 錫良
Xiong Xiling 熊希齡
Xu Dinglin 許鼎霖
Xu Shiying 許世英
Xu Shichang 徐世昌
Xu Zhen 徐珍
Xuantong 宣統
xunfangdui 巡防隊
xunjing 巡警
xunjin zongjuzhang 巡警総局長

yamen 衙門
Yan Panchun 焉泮春
Yangwu yungdong 洋務運動
yishihui 議事会
Yokohama Shōkin 横浜正金
yongdian quan 永佃権
Yongling 永陵
Yu Chonghan 于冲漢
Yu Lu 裕禄
yuan 元
Yuan Jinkai 袁金鎧
Yuan Shikai 袁世凱
Yuan Zhennan 袁鎮南

zaobichang zongban 造幣廠総辦
Zeng Youyi 曾有翼
Zhang Chenyi 張臣翼
Zhang Geren 張根仁
Zhang Gui 張桂
Zhang Huanbai 張煥柏
Zhang Huanxiang 張煥相
Zhang Huanyu 張煥棫
Zhang Huijing 張惠景
Zhang Qinshan 張欽善
Zhang Rong 張榕
Zhang Shaozeng 張紹曾
Zhang Xiluan 張錫鑾
Zhang Xueliang 張学良
Zhang Yuanqi 張元奇
Zhang Zuolin 張作霖
Zhao Erxun 趙爾巽
Zhaoling 昭陵
Zhaoling yaochai guandiandi 昭陵

窯柴官甸地
zhengbai 正白
zhenghong 正紅
zhenghuang 正黄
zhenglan 正藍
zhengshen qiren 正身旗人
Zhengzhi guanbao 政治官報
zhifu 知府
zhizheng 執政
zhou 州
zhuangding 荘丁
zhuangtou 荘頭
ziyiju 諮議局
zizhengyuan 資政院
Ziyiju choubanchu 諮議局籌辦処
Ziyiju lianhehui 諮議局聯合会
Zizhi qichenghui 自治期成会
Zizhi yanjiusuo 自治研究所
zongdu 総督
zu 租

Bibliography

Unless otherwise indicated, all Japanese publishers are located in Tokyo.

Ajia Keizai Kenkyūjo アジア経済研究所, ed. *Kyū shokuminchi kankei kikan kankōbutsu sōgō mokuroku—Manshūkoku Kantō-chō hen*—旧植民地関係機関刊行物総合目録—満洲国関東庁編 (Union catalogue of publications of the former colonial institutions: Manzhouguo government and the Japanese colonial authority of the Guandong Leased Territory). Ajia Keizai Kenkyūjo, 1975.

———. *Kyū shokuminchi kankei kikan kankōbutsu sōgō mokuroku—Minami Manshū Tetsudō Kabushiki Kaisha hen*—旧植民地関係機関刊行物総合目録—南満洲鉄道株式会社編— (Union catalogue of publications of the former colonial institutions: The South Manchuria Railroad Company). Ajia Keizai Kenkyūjo, 1979.

Amagai Kenzaburō 天海謙三郎. *Naimufu kanshō* 内務府官荘 (Manors of the Imperial Household Department). Dairen: Minami Manshū Tetsudō Kabushiki Kaisha, 1914.

———. *Kōsan* 皇産 (Lands owned by the Qing court). Dairen: Minami Manshū Tetsudō Kabushiki Kaisha, 1915.

———. *Suichūken Ryōkaton kanshō shōkachi chōsa hōkoku-sho* 綏中縣凌家屯官荘升科地調查報告書 (Report of an investigation of the former public manor lands in Lingjiatun, Suizhong County). Tochi Seido Chōsa-kai, 1939.

———. *Chūgoku tochi monjo no kenkyū* 中国土地文書の研究 (Studies of Chinese documents on land). Keisō Shobō, 1966.

Amano Motonosuke 天野元之助. *Manshū keizai no hattatsu* 満洲経済の発達 (The development of the Manchurian economy). Dairen: Minami Manshū Tetsudō Kabushiki Kaisha, 1932.

Anami Koretaka 阿南惟高. "Hakki" 八旗 (Eight Banners). In *Ajia rekishi jiten* アジア歴史事典 (Encyclopedia of Asian history), vol. 7, 384–85. Heibonsha, 1961.

Chang P'eng-yüan 張朋園. *Lixian pai yu Xinhai geming* 立憲派與辛亥革命 (Constitutionalists and the 1911 Revolution). Taipei: Zhongguo xueshu zhuzuo jiangzhu weiyuanhui, 1969.

Chao Chung-fu 趙中孚. "Qingdai Dongsansheng yimin wenti zhi yanjiu" 清代東三省移民問題之研究 (Immigration and the agricultural development of Manchuria: A case study of inter-regional migration in China). *Zhongyang yanjiuyuan jindai shi yanjiusuo qikan* 中央研究院近代史研究所期刊 4,下 (1974): 613–64.

———. "Qingmo Dongsansheng gaizhi de beijing" 清末東三省改制的背景 (Manchuria: The frontier government and its reorganization). *Zhongyang yanjiuyuan jindai shi yanjiusuo qikan* 中央研究院近代史研究所期刊 5 (1976): 313–35.

———. "Qingdai Dongsansheng gufei wenti zhi tantao" 清代東三省股匪問題之探討 (Frontier outlaws in Manchuria, 1890–1930). *Zhongyang yanjiuyuan jindai shi yanjiusuo qikan* 中央研究院近代史研究所期刊 7 (1978): 509–25.

———. "The Role of the Government in Inner-regional Migration and Agricultural Development: A Case Study of Manchuria, 1668–1911." *Zhongyang yanjiuyuan jindai shi yanjiusuo qikan* 中央研究院近代史研究所期刊 9 (1979): 255–68.

———. "Jindai Dongsansheng de diquan yu fengjin zhengce" 近代東三省的地權與封禁政策 (Land tenure in Manchuria: Myth and reality of the "forbidden territory"). *Zhongyang yanjiuyuan jindai shi yanjiusuo qikan* 中央研究院近代史研究所期刊 10 (1980): 283–302.

———. "Xinhai geming qianhou de Dongsansheng" 辛亥革命前後的東三省 (Manchuria before and after the 1911 Revolution). *Zhongyang yanjiuyuan jindai shi yanjiusuo qikan* 中央研究院近代史研究所期刊 11 (1981): 117–30.

———. *Jinshi Dongsansheng yanjiu lunwen ji* 近世東三省研究論文集 (Studies on Dongsansheng in the modern period). Taipei: Chengwen chubanshe, 1999.

Chen Jiahua 陳佳華, and Fu Kedong 傅克東. "Baqi jianli qian niulu renkou chutan" 八旗建立前牛彔人口初探 (A preliminary investigation into Manchurian Niulu and its population before the establishment of the Eight Banner system). In *Manzu shi yanjiuji* 滿族史研究集 (Collected works in the study of Manchu history), edited by Wang Zhonghan 王鍾翰, 259–80. Beijing: Zhongguo shehui kexue chubanshe, 1988.

———. "Baqi hanjun kaolüe" 八旗漢軍考略 (A study of the Han Banners). In *Manzu shi yanjiuji* 滿族史研究集 (Collected works in the study of Manchu history), edited by Wang Zhonghan 王鍾翰, 281–306. Beijing: Zhongguo shehui kexue chubanshe, 1988.

Cheng Qilu 程起陸. "Guanwai geming huiyilu" 關外革命回憶錄 (Memoir of the revolution in Manchuria). In *Xinhai geming huiyilu* 辛亥革命回憶 (Memoirs of the 1911 Revolution), edited by Zhongguo renmin zhengzhi xieshang huiyi quanguo weiyuanhui wenshi shiliao yanjiu weiyuanhui, vol. 5, 560–65. Beijing: Zhonghua shudian, 1963.

Crossley, Pamela Kyle. *Orphan Warriors: Three Manchu Generations and the End of the Qing Dynasty.* Princeton: Princeton University Press, 1990.

Dazai Matsusaburō 太宰松三郎. *Manshū gendai shi* 満洲現代史 (A contemporary history of Manchuria). Dairen: Minami Manshū Tetsudō Kabushiki Kaisha, 1923.

Dengta xianzhi 灯塔県志 (Local gazetteer of Dengta County). Compiled by Dengta xianzhi bangongshi. Shenyang: Liaoning renmin chubanshe, 1990.

DesForges, Roger. *Hsi-liang and the Chinese National Revolution.* New Haven: Yale University Press, 1973.

Dongbei nianjian, Minguo 20 nian ban 東北年鑑, 民国二十年版 (A yearbook of Northeast Provinces, 1931 edition). Shenyang: Dongbei wenhuashe, 1931.

Ding Yizhuang 定宜庄, Guo Songyi 郭松義, Li Zhongqing 李中清, and Kang Wenlin 康文林. *Liaodong yimin zhong de qiren shehui: Lishi wenxian, renkou tongji yu tianye diaocha* 遼東移民中的旗人社会: 歴史文献, 人口統計与田野調査 (Banner society among immigrants in Liaodong: Historical documents, population data, and field surveys). Forthcoming.

Dongfang zazhi 東方雑誌 (Eastern Miscellany). Shangwuyin shuguan, 1904–1948. Reprint, 44 vols. Taipei: Taiwan shangwuyin shuguan, 1973.

Elliott, Mark. "The Limits of Tartary: Manchuria in Imperial and National Geographies." *Journal of Asian Studies* 59.3 (2000): 603–4.

———. *The Manchu Way: The Eight Banners and Ethnic Identity in Late Imperial China.* Stanford: Stanford University Press, 2001.

Enatsu Yoshiki 江夏由樹. "Shindai no jidai, Tōsanshō ni okeru hakki shōen no sōtō ni tsuite no ichi kōsatsu" 清朝の時代、東三省における八旗荘園の荘頭についての一考察 (An study of Manchu manor managers in the Three Eastern Provinces during the Qing period). *Shakai Keizaishigaku* 社会経済史学 46.1 (1980): 59–76.

———. "Shinmatsu no jiki, Tōsanshō nanbu ni okeru kanchi no jōhō no shakai keizaishi teki imi" 清末の時期、東三省南部における官地の丈放の社会経済史的意味 (The social-economic significance of the disposition of official land in southern Dongsansheng at the end of the Qing dynasty). *Shakai Keizaishigaku* 社会経済史学 49.4 (1983): 28–47.

———. "Kantō Totoku-fu oyobi Kantō-chō no tochi chōsa jigyō ni tsuite" 関東都督府及び関東庁の土地調査事業について (The land survey by Kantō Totoku-fu and Kantō-chō). *Hitotsubashi Ronsō* 一橋論叢 97.3 (1987): 85–102.

———. "Shingai kakumei go, kyū Hōtensho ni okeru kan'yūchi no haraisage ni tsuite" 辛亥革命後、旧奉天省における官有地の払い下げについて (The disposition of official land in Fengtian Province after the 1911 Revolution). *Hitotsubashi Ronsō* 一橋論叢 98.6 (1987): 23–42.

———. "Kyū Kinshū kanshō no sōtō to eidenko" 旧錦州官荘の荘頭と永佃戸 (Manager and permanent tenants of the former Jinzhou manors). *Shakai Keizaishigaku* 社会経済史学 54.6 (1989): 1–27.

———. "Hōten chihō kanryō shūdan no keisei" 奉天地方官僚集団の形成 (The formation of a Fengtian local bureaucratic clique). *Keizaigaku Kenkyū* 経済学研究 31 (1990): 309–47.

———. "Shingai kakumei go kyū Hōten-shō ni okeru kanchi no haraisage" 辛亥革命後、旧奉天省における官地の払い下げ (The disposition of official land in Fengtian after the 1911 Revolution). *Tōyōshi Kenkyū* 東洋史研究 53.3 (1994): 103–27.

———. "Tochi riken o meguru Chūgoku Nihon no kanmin kankei" 土地利権をめぐる中国日本の官民関係 (Land rights and Chinese and Japanese bureaucrats and politicians). *Ajia keizai* アジア経済 38.1 (1997): 2–24.

———. "Chūgoku Tōhoku chiikishi kenkyū to tōan shiryō" 中国東北地域史研究と档案史料 (A study of the local history and archives of Northeastern China with reference to local administration and land affairs). *Tōyōshi Kenkyū* 東洋史研究 58.3 (1999): 173–93.

———. "Establishment of the Modern Land System in Fengtian (Southern Manchuria) at the Beginning of the Twentieth Century: Development of Land Market in Manchuria." *The Memoirs of the Toyo Bunko* 52 (2001): 87–107.

Esherick, Joseph W. *Reform and Revolution in China*. Berkeley: University of California Press, 1976.

Esherick, Joseph W., and Mary Backus Rankin, eds. *Chinese Local Elites and Patterns of Dominance*. Berkeley: University of California Press, 1990.

Fengtian nongshi shiyanchang 奉天農事試験場, ed. *Fengtian quansheng nongye diaocha shu* 奉天全省農業調査書 (Report of an investigation of agriculture in Fengtian Province). Fengtian, 1909.

Fengtian tongzhi 奉天通志 (Local gazetteer of Fengtian). Compiled by Wang Shunan 王樹楠 et al., 260 *juan*, 1934. Reprinted in 5 vols. Shenyang: Shengyang gujiu shudian, 1983.

Fujii Masao 藤井正夫. "Manshūkoku" 満州国 (Manzhouguo). In *Chūgokushi kenkyū nyūmon* 中国史研究入門 (Introduction to the study of Chinese history), edited by Yamane Yukio 山根幸夫, vol. 2, 433–41. Yamakawa Shuppan, 1983.

Fujii Ryō 藤井遼. *Manshū ni okeru Shina ginkō no gaiyō* 満洲における支那銀行の概要 (An outline of Chinese banks in Manchuria). Dairen: Minami Manshū Tetsudō Kabushiki Kaisha, 1929.

Gaimushō Jōhō-bu 外務省情報部, ed. *Gendai Chūka Minkoku, Manshū teikoku jinmeikan, Shōwa 12 nen ban* 現代中華民国, 滿洲帝国人名鑑, 昭和 12 年版 (A directory of important people in contemporary Republic of China and Manzhouguo, 1937 edition). Tōa Dōbunkai, 1937.

———. *Gendai Shina jinmeikan* 現代支那人名鑑 (A directory of contemporary Chinese). Tokyo, 1924.

Gottschang, Thomas R. and Diana Lary. *Swallows and Settlers: The Great Migration from North China to Manchuria*. Ann Arbor: Center for Chinese Studies, University of Michigan, 2000.

Gugong bowuyuan Ming-Qing dang'anbu 故宮博物院明清档案部, ed. *Guanyu Jiangning zhizao Caojia dang'an shiliao* 関與江寧織造曹家档案史料 (Historical materials concerning the Cao family of the Jiangning textile commission). Beijing: Zhonghua shuju, 1975.

Hailong xianzhi 海龍縣志 (Local gazetteer of Hailong County). Compiled by Bai Yongzhen 白永貞 et al., 1913.

He Donglin 何東林. "Xinhai geming zai Liaoyang" 辛亥革命在遼陽 (The 1911 Revolution in Liaoyang). In *Xinhai geming huiyilu* 辛亥革命回憶録 (Memoirs of the 1911 Revolution), edited by Zhongguo renmin zhengzhi xieshang huiyi quanguo weiyuanhui wenshi shiliao yanjiu weiyuanhui, vol. 5, 566–71. Beijing: Zhonghua shudian, 1963.

Hosoya Yoshio 細谷良夫. "Manju Gurun to Manshūkoku" マンジュグルンと滿洲国 (Manju gurun and Manzhouguo). In *Rekishi no naka no chiiki* 歴史のなかの地域 (Regions in history), edited by Shibata Michio et al., 105–36. Iwanami Shoten, 1990.

Hummel, Arthur W. *Eminent Chinese of the Ch'ing Period (1644–1912)*. Washington, D.C.: United States Government Printing Office, 1944.

Imura Tetsurō 井村哲郎. "Manshūkoku kankei shiryō kaidai" 滿洲国関係資料解題 (Bibliographical introduction for the study of Manzhouguo). In *Manshūkoku no kenkyū* 滿洲国の研究 (The study of Manzhouguo), edited by Yamamoto Yūzō 山本有造, 535–80. Kyoto: Kyōto University, 1993.

Inaba Iwakichi 稲葉岩吉. *Zōtei Manshū hattatsu shi* 増訂滿洲発達史 (The history of the development of Manchuria, expanded edition). Nihon Hyōronsha, 1935.

Ishibashi Takao 石橋崇雄. *Daishin teikoku* 大清帝国 (The Great Qing empire). Kōdansha, 2000.

Ishida Kōhei [石田興平]. *Manshū ni okeru shokuminchi keizai no shiteki tenkai* 滿洲における植民地経済の史的展開 (The history of the development of Manchuria's colonial economy). Kyoto: Mineruba Shobō, 1964.

Kamebuchi Ryuchō 亀淵龍長. *Mōchi* 蒙地 (Land held by Mongols). Dairen: Minami Manshū Tetsudō Kabushiki Kaisha, 1914.

———. *Ippan Minchi: jō, chū, ge* 一般民地—上、中、下 (Civil land, vols. 1–3). Dairen: Minami Manshū Tetsudō Kabushiki Kaisha, 1914–1915.

Kanda Nobuo 神田信夫. "Shin no kōki" 清の興起 (The rise of the Qing). In *Sekai rekishi taikei, Chūgokushi* 4 世界歴史体系, 中国史 4 (World history, Chinese history 4), edited by Matsumaru Michio et al., 295–318. Yamakawa Shuppansha, 1999.

Kanda Nobuo 神田信夫, and Hosoya Yoshio 細谷良夫. "Shindai" 清代 (The Qing period). In *Chūgokushi kenkyū nyūmon* 中国史研究入門 (Introduction to the study of Chinese history), edited by Yamane Yukio 山根幸夫, vol. 2, 91–105. Yamakawa Shuppan, 1983.

Kaneko Fumio 金子文夫. "1970 nendai ni okeru Manshū kenkyū no jōkyō" 1970 年代における『満州』研究の状況 (The present state of the study of Manchuria in the 1970s). *Ajia Keizai* アジア経済 20.3 (1979): 38–55; 20.11 (1979): 24–43.

Kantō Totoku-fu 関東都督府, ed. *Manshū chihō-shi* 満洲地方誌 (Compilation of surveys conducted by the Japan's governor-general office in Lüshun). Kantō Totoku-fu, 1911.

———. *Manshū ippan-shi sōkō* 満洲一般誌草稿 (General history of Manchuria, manuscript). Kantō Totoku-fu, 1911.

Katō Shigeshi 加藤繁. "Kandai ni okeru kokka zaisei to teishitsu zaisei tono kubetsu narabini teishitu zaisei ippan" 漢代における国家財政と帝室財政との区別並びに帝室財政一斑 (Distinction between governmental finances and Imperial Household finances and a general explanation about Imperial Household finances). In *Shina keizaishi kōshō* 支那経済史考証 (Studies on Chinese economic history), by Katō Shigeshi, 2 vols. Tōyō Bunko, 1953.

Kessker, Lawrence. *K'ang-hsi and the Consolidation of Ch'ing Rule 1661–1684*. Chicago: Chicago University Press, 1976.

Kuhn, Philip. *Rebellion and Its Enemies in Late Imperial China*. Cambridge, Mass.: Harvard University Press, 1970.

Lee, James, and Cameron Campbell. *Fate and Fortune in Rural China: Social Organization and Population Behavior in Liaoning, 1774–1873*. Cambridge: Cambridge University Press, 1997.

Lee, Robert H. G. *The Manchurian Frontier in Ch'ing History*. Cambridge, Mass.: Harvard University Press, 1970.

Li Shiyue 李時岳. "Xinhai geming shiqi, Dongsansheng geming yu fan geming de douzheng" 辛亥革命時期、東三省革命与反革命的闘争 (The struggle between revolutionaries and anti-revolutionaries in Dongsansheng at the time of the 1911 Revolution). *Lishi yanjiu* 歴史研究 1959.6 (1959): 56–70.

Li Shou-k'ung 李守孔. "Gesheng ziyiju lianhehui yu Xinhai geming" 各省諮議局連合会与辛亥革命 (Association of Provincial Assemblies and the 1911 Revolution). In *Zhongguo xiandai shi congkan* 中国現代史叢刊 (Studies in the history of contemporary China), edited by Wu Hsiang-hsiang 呉湘相, vol. 3, 321–73. Taipei: Zhengzhong shuju, 1962.

Li Wenzhi 李文治, ed. *Zhongguo jindai nongye shi ziliao* 中国近代農業史資料 (Collected sources of agricultural history in modern China). Beijing: Sanlian shudian, 1957.

Liang Fangzhong 梁方仲. *Zhongguo lidai hukou tiandi tianbu tongji* 中国歴代戸口田地田賦統計 (Historical statistics for the population, households, acreage of arable lands, and land taxation in China). Shanghai: Shanghai renmin chubanshe, 1980.

Liaoning sheng dang'anguan 遼寧省档案館, ed. "Xinhai geming zai Fengtian" 辛亥革命在奉天 (The 1911 Revolution in Fengtian Province). *Lishi dang'an* 歴史档案 1981.4 (1981): 17–29.

———. *Xinhai geming zai Lioaning dang'an shiliao* 辛亥革命在遼寧档案史料 (Archival materials concerning the 1911 Revolution in Liaoning). Shenyang: Liaoningshen dang'anguan, 1981.

———. *Shengjing neiwufu liangzhuang dang'an huibian* 盛京内務府粮庄档案彙編 (Collected *dang'an* materials about manors of the Shengjing Neiwufu), 2 vols. Shenyang: Liaoshen shushe, 1993.

Liaoyang shizhi 遼陽市志 (Gazetteer of Liaoyang City), compiled by Liaoyang shizhi bianzuan weiyuanhui. Shenyang: Liaoning renmin chubanshe, 1993.

Liaoyang xianzhi 遼陽縣志 (Gazetteer of Liaoyang County), compiled by Fei Huanxing 斐煥星 et al. 40 *juan*, 1928. Reprinted in 5 vols. Taipei: Chengwen chubanshe, 1973.

Liaoyang xianzhi 遼陽県志 (Local gazetteer of Liaoyang County), compiled by Liaoyang xianzhi bianzuan weiyuanhui. Anshan: Xinhua chubanshe, 1994.

Liu Shoulin 劉寿林. *Xinhai yihou shiqi nian zhiguan nianbiao* 辛亥以後17年職官年表 (Chronological table of officials in the 17 years following the 1911 Revolution). Beijing: Zhonghua shudian, 1960.

McCormack, Gavan. *Chang Tso-lin in Northeast China 1911–1928*. Stanford: Stanford University Press, 1977.

Manbun Rōtō Kenkyūkai 満文老档研究会. *Manbun rōtō* 満文老档 (Japanese translation of *Manwen laodang*). Tōyō Bunko, 1959.

(Manshūkoku) Kokumuin Jitsugyōbu Rinji Sangyō Chōsakyoku (満洲国) 国務院実業部臨時産業調査局, ed. *Kōtoku gannendo nōson jittai chōsa hōkoku-sho kobetu chōsa no bu,* 康徳元年度 農村実態調査報告書, 戸別調査の部 (Report of the actual state of agricultural villages, door-to-door inquiry, Kōtoku first-year edition), 3 vols. Shinkyō, 1935.

(Manshūkoku) Kokumuin Jitsugyōbu Rinji Sangyō Chōsakyoku (満洲国) 国務院実業部臨時産業調査局, ed. *Kōtoku 3 nendo nōson jittai chōsa hōkoku-sho kobetu chōsa no bu*, 康徳 3 年度 農村実態調査報告書, 戸別調査の部 (Report of the actual state of agricultural villages, door-to-door inquiry, Kōtoku third-year edition), 4 vols. Shinkyō, 1936.

(Manshūkoku) Kokumuin Sangyōbu Nōmushi (満洲国) 国務院産業部農務司, ed. *Kōtoku 4 nendo Kengishi minaraisei nōson jittai chōsa hōkoku-sho, Kinshū-shō Suichū-ken* 康徳 4 年度 縣技士見習生農村実態調査報告書, 錦州省綏中縣 (Report of the actual state of agricultural villages by officials in training, Suizhong County, Jinzhou Province, Kōtoku fourth-year edition). Shinkyō, 1938.

(Manshūkoku) Kokumuin Tōkei Hensan-sho 満洲国国務院統計編纂所, ed. *Dai 1 ji manshūkoku nenpō* 第一次満洲国年報 (First annual report on Manzhouguo). Shinkyō: Kokumuin Tōkei-sho, 1933.

Manshūkoku Tochikyoku 満洲国土地局. *Manshū ni okeru tochi seido no gaiyō* 満洲における土地制度の概要 (An overview of the land system in Manchuria). Shinkyō, 1935.

Masubuchi Tatsuo 増渕龍夫. "Rekishi ninshiki ni okeru shōko shugi to genjitsu hihan" 歴史認識における尚古主義と現実批判 (Classicism and critique of reality in the understanding of history). In *Rekishi-ka no dōjidai-shi teki kōsatsu ni tsuite* 歴史家の同時代的考察について (Historians' investigation into contemporary history), by Masubuchi Tatsuo, 171–224. Iwanami Shoten, 1983.

Minami Manshū Tetsudō Kabushiki Kaisha Chōsabu 南満洲鉄道株式会社調査部, ed. *Chūgoku nōson kankō chōsa* 中国農村慣行調査 (Investigation of customs in Chinese villages), 6 vols. Reprint. Iwanami Shoten, 1981.

Mitamura Taisuke 三田村泰助. *Shinchō zenshi no kenkyū* 清朝前史の研究 (Study on pre-Qing history). Kyoto: Tōyōshi Kenkyūkai, 1965.

Miyauchi Kishi 宮内季子. *Ō no kanshū* 押の慣習 (The customs of Ya). Dairen: Minami Manshū Tetsudō Kabushiki Kaisha, 1913.

———. *Ten no kanshū* 典の慣習 (The customs of Dian). Dairen: Minami Manshū Tetsudō Kabushiki Kaisha, 1913.

Muramatsu Yūji 村松祐次. "Kenryū jidai kakyū Manshū kizoku no chisan to jintei" 乾隆時代下級満洲貴族の地産と人丁 (Land and peasants of the lower Manchu nobles during the Qianlong period). *Tōyōshi Kenkyū* 東洋史研究 28.4 (1970): 75–98.

Myers, Ramon. *The Chinese Peasant Economy: Agricultural Development in Hopei and Shantung, 1840–1940*. Cambridge, Mass.: Harvard University Press, 1970.

Nakami Tatsuo 中見立夫. "Chiiki gainen no seijisei" 地域概念の政治性 (The politics of the concept of region). In *Kōsakusuru Azia* 交錯するアジア (The mutual involvement of Asia) edited by Mizoguchi Yūzō 溝口雄三 et al., 273–95. Tōkyō Daigaku Shuppan-kai, 1993.

Narakino Shimesu 楢木野宣. *Shindai jūyō shokkan no kenkyū* 清代重要職官の研究 (A study on significant posts in the Qing government). Kazama Shobō, 1975.

Neiwufu (清)内務府. *Guochao jianye chuji jilüe* 国朝建業初基紀略 (Brief history on the first basis for the foundation of the dynasty). Reprint, 2 vols. Beijing: Beijing University Press, 1993.

Ning Wu 寧武. "Dongbei Xinhai geming jianshu" 東北辛亥革命簡述 (A brief summary of the 1911 Revolution in Manchuria). In *Xinhai geming huiyilu* 辛亥革命回憶録 (Memoirs of the 1911 Revolution), edited by Zhongguo renmin zhengzhi xieshang huiyi quanguo weiyuanhui wenshi shiliao yanjiu weiyuanhui, vol. 5, 536–59. Beijing: Zhonghua shudian, 1963.

Nishimura Shigeo 西村成雄. "Tōsanshō ni okeru Shingai Kakumei" 東三省における辛亥革命 (The 1911 Revolution in Manchuria). *Rekishigaku Kenkyū* 歴史学研究 358 (1970): 12–30.

———. *Chūgoku kindai Tōhoku chiikishi kenkyū* 中国近代東北地域史研究 (Historical studies on modern Northeast China). Kyoto: Hōritsu Bunkasha, 1984.

Oda Yorozu 織田萬 et al., eds. *Shinkoku gyōsei-hō* 清国行政法 (Qing administrative law). Kobe: Rinji Taiwan Kyūkan Chōsa-kai, 1905–1914. Reprint, 7 vols. Kyūko Shoin, 1972.

Oshino Akio 押野昭生. "Ryōyō" 遼陽 (Liaoyang). In *Ajia rekishi jiten* アジア歴史事典 (Encyclopedia of Asian History), vol. 9, 308. Heibonsha, 1960.

Ōtani Takeo 大谷武夫. "Shinshikō no seiritsu to sono seikaku" 清史稿の成立とその性格 (Compilation of a draft of Qing history and its features). Mantetsu Chōsa Geppō 満鉄調査月報 22.9 (1942): 171–82.

Pekin Shina Kenkyūkai 北京支那研究会, ed. *Saishin Shina kanshin-roku* 最新支那官紳録 (The latest directory of Chinese officials). Beijing: Shina Kenkyūkai, 1918.

Perry, Elizabeth. *Rebels and Revolutionaries in North China*. Stanford: Stanford University Press, 1980.

Qian Shifu 銭実甫. *Qingji xinshe zhiguan nianbiao* 清季新設職官年表 (Chronological table of new posts in the Qing government). Beijing: Zhonghua shuju, 1961.

Qin Chengzhi 秦誠至. "Xinhai geming yu Zhang Rong" 辛亥革命與張榕 (The 1911 Revolution and Zhang Rong). In *Xinhai geming huiyilui* 辛亥革命回憶録 (Memoirs of the 1911 Revolution), edited by Zhongguo renmin zhengzhi xieshang huiyi quanguo weiyuanhui wenshi shiliao yanjiu weiyuanhui, vol. 5, 592–611. Beijing: Zhonghua shudian, 1963.

Rankin, Mary. *Elite Activism and Political Transformation in China*. Stanford: Stanford University Press, 1986.

Rhoads, Edward J. M. *Manchus and Han*. Seattle: University of Washington Press, 2000.

Sanbō Honbu 参謀本部. *Meiji 37, 38 nen Nichiro sensō-shi* 明治 37, 38 年日露戦争史 (History of the Russo-Japanese War, 1904–1905). Tokyo Kaikōsha, 1912.

Shengjing shibao 盛京時報 (The Shengjing Times). Shengjing Shibaoshe, 1906–?.

Shenyang shi dang'anguan 瀋陽市档案館, ed. *Xinhai geming zai Shenyang* 辛亥革命在瀋陽 (The 1911 Revolution in Shenyang). Shenyang: Shenyang chubanshe, 1991.

Sonoda Kazuki 園田一亀. *Hōtenha no shinjin to kyūjin* 奉天派の新人と旧人 (New and old generations of the Fengtian political group). Fengtian: Manshū Nichi-nichi Shinbunsha, 1922.

———. Hōtenshō zaisei no kenkyū 奉天省財政の研究 (A study of the finances of Fengtian Province). Fengtian: Hōtenjihō-sha, 1927.

Spence, Jonathan. *Ts'ao Yin and the K'ang-hsi Emperor.* New Haven: Yale University Press, 1965.

Sudō Yoshiyuki 周藤吉之. *Shindai Manshū tochi seisaku no kenkyū* 清代満洲土地政策の研究 (A study of Qing land policy in Manchuria). Kawade Shobō, 1944.

———. "Shinchō shoki ni okeru tōjū to sono kigen" 清朝初期における投充とその起源 (The surrender of Han Chinese to the Manchu and its origin at the beginning of the Qing period). In *Shindai Higashi Ajia-shi kenkyū* 清代東アジア史研究 (Study on East Asian history during the Qing period), by Sudō Yoshiyuki, 1–107. Nihon Gakujutsu Shinkōkai, 1972.

Sugata Kumaemon 眇田熊衛門. *Soken* 租権 (Rights of Zu). Dairen: Minami Manshū Tetsudō Kabushiki Kaisha, 1913.

Sun Jiagan 孫嘉淦. "Baqi gongchan shu" 八旗公產疏 (Memorials regarding the Eight Banner lands). In *Huangchao jingshi wenbian* 皇朝経世文編, *juan* 35.10b–11a. Reprinted in *Jindai Zhongguo shiliao congkan* 近代中国史料叢刊, edited by Shen Yunlong 沈雲龍 et al., sec. 74, vol 3. Taipei: Wenhai chubanshe, 1964.

Suzuki Takashi 鈴木隆. "Manshū kenkyū no genjō to kadai" 満洲研究の現状と課題 (The present state of and issues in the study of Manchuria). *Ajia Keizai* アジア経済 12.4 (1971): 49–60.

Tahara Teijirō 田原禎二郎. *Shinmatsu minsho Chūgoku kanshin jinmeiroku* 清末民初中国官紳人名録 (A directory of Chinese officials at the end of the Qing and the beginning of the Republican period). Beijing: Chūgoku Kenkyūkai, 1918.

Tamura Jitsuzō 田村実造. *Chūgoku seifuku ōchō no kenkyū* 中国征服王朝の研究 (Studies of conqueror dynasties in China), vol. 1. Kyoto: Tōyōshi Kenkyūkai, 1964.

Tanabe Tanejirō 田邊種治郎. *Tōsanshō kanshin-roku* 東三省官紳録 (A directory of officials in the Three Eastern Provinces). Dairen: Tōsanshō Kanshin-roku Kankōkai, 1924.

Ukon 右近. "Manshū tōchi to jinushi kaikyū" 満洲統治と地主階級 (The governing of Manchuria and the landlord class). *Manshū Hyōron* 満洲評論 8.2 (1935): 2–3.

Ura Ren'ichirō 浦廉一郎. "Kangun (Ujen Cooha) ni tsuite" 漢軍 (Ujen Cooha) について (A study of Han bannermen). In *Kuwabara hakase kanreki kinen tōyōshi ronsō* 桑原博士還暦記念東洋史論叢 (Studies of Oriental history contributed in celebration of the sixtieth birthday of Professor Kuwabara), 815–49. Kōbundō, 1930.

Wada Kiyoshi 和田清. *Chūgoku chihō jichi hattatsu-shi (Eiin-ban)* 中国地方自治発達史, 影印版 (History of the development of self-government in China, reprint edition). Kyūko Shoin, 1975.

Wang Gesheng 王革生. *Qingdai Dongbei tudi zhidushi* 清代東北土地制度史 (History of the land system in Manchuria during the Qing period). Shengyang: Lioaning daxue chubanshe, 1991.

Wang Kuixi 王魁喜, Wu Wenxian 王文銜, Lu Fang 陸方, Shi Zhen 石箴, Xu Feng 徐楓, and Xu Fengchen 徐風晨. *Jindai Dongbei shi* 近代東北史 (Modern Manchurian history). Haerbin: Heilongjiang renmin chubanshe, 1984.

Wang Zhonghan 王鍾翰, ed. *Manzu shi yanjiu ji* 满族史研究集 (Collected works in the study of Manchu history). Beijing: Zhongguo shehui kexue chubanshe, 1988.

———. "Guanyu Manzu xingcheng zhong de jige wenti" 関與満族形成中的幾個問題 (Some issues in the formation of the Manchu people). In *Manzu shi yanjiu ji* 满族史研究集 (Collected works in the study of Manchu history), edited by Wang Zhonghan 王鍾翰, 1–16. Beijing: Zhongguo shehui kexue chubanshe, 1988.

Watanuki Tetsurō 綿貫哲郎. "Shinsho no kyūkanjin to hakki kangun" 清初の旧漢人と八旗漢軍 (Former Han civilians and Han bannermen). *Shisō* 史叢 67 (2002): 31–41.

Xinhai geming huiyilu 辛亥革命回憶録 (Memoirs of the 1911 Revolution). Edited by Zhongguo renmin zhengzhi xieshang huiyi quanguo weiyuanhui wenshi shiliao yanjiu weiyuanhui 中国人民政治協商会議全国委員会文史資料研究委員会.Vol. 5. Beijing: Zhonghua shudian, 1963.

Xu Shichang 徐世昌. *Tuigengtang congshu* 退耕堂叢書 (Collected works of Tuigengtang). In *Jindai Zhongguo shiliao congkan* 近代中国史料叢刊, edited by Shen Yunlong 沈雲龍 et al., sec. 23. Reprinted in 5 vols. Taipei: Wenhai chubanshe, 1964.

———. *Dongsansheng zhenglüe* 東三省政略 (The administration of the Three Eastern Provinces). Reprinted in 12 vols. Taipei: Chengwen chubanshe, 1965.

Yamaguchi Shigetsugu 山口重次. Kieta teikoku Manshū 消えた帝国満洲 (Manzhouguo, the empire that disappeared). Mainichi Shinbunsha, 1967.

Yamane Yukio 山根幸夫, ed. *Chūgokushi kenkyū nyūmon* 中国史研究入門 (Introduction to the study of Chinese history), 2 vols. Yamakawa Shuppan, 1983.

Yi Baozhong 衣保中 et al., eds. *Qingdai Manzhou tudi zhidu yanjiu* 清代満洲土地制度研究 (A study of the land system in Manchuria during the Qing period). Jilin: Jilin shifan guji yanjiusuo, 1993.

Yoshida Kin'ichi 吉田金一. "Ba Senzan" 馬占山 (Ma Zhanshan). In *Ajia rekishi jiten* アジア歴史事典 (Encyclopedia of Asian history), vol. 7, 374. Heibonsha, 1960.

Yuan Jinkai 袁金鎧. *Yonglu riji yucun fu jingguo zishu* 傭廬日記語存附経過自述 (Diary of Yonglu). Deposited at the Liaoning Provincial Library, Shenyang.

Yuan Qingxuan 袁慶璇. "Yuan Jinkai nianpu" 袁金鎧年譜 (Chronological record of Yuan Jinkai). In *Liaoyang wenshi ziliao* 遼陽文史資料, edited by Zhengxie Liaoyangshi wenshi ziliao weiyuanhui, vol. 6, 151–61. Liaoyang: Liaoyang wenshi ziliao chubanshe, 1992.

Zhang Xia 張俠, Sun Baoming 孫宝銘, and Chen Zhanghe 陳長河, eds. *Beiyang lujun shiliao* 北洋陸軍史料, 1912–1916 (Historical sources of the Beiyang Army, 1912–1916). Tianjin: Tianjin renmin chubanshe, 1982.

Zhao Erxun 趙爾巽 et al., eds. *Qingshi gao* 清史稿 (Draft history of the Qing), 485 *juan*. Reprinted in 48 vols. Beijing: Zhonghua shuju, 1984.

Zhi Xin 直心, and Gui Dong 桂冬. "Yuan Jinkai de yisheng" 袁金鎧的一生 (The life of Yuan Jinkai). In *Liaoyang wenshi ziliao* 遼陽文史資料, edited by Liaoyangshi zhengxie wenshi ziliao weiyuanhui, vol. 7, 166–96. Liaoyang, 1994.

Zhongguo diyi lishi dang'anguan 中国第一歴史档案館, ed. *Qingdai dang'an shiliao congpian, di 8 ji: Dongsansheng Xinhai geming shiliao* 清代档案史料叢編,第八集: 東三省辛亥革命史料 (Collection of *dang'an* materials in the Qing period, vol. 8: Historical materials on the 1911 Revolution in Dongsansheng). Beijing: Zhonghua shudian, 1982.

Zhongguo fangzhi congshu 中国方志叢書: *Dongbei difang* 東北地方 (A collection of local gazetteers of China: The Northeast). Taipei: Chengwen chubanshe, 1973.

Zhongguo kexueyuan Jilin sheng fenyuan lishi yanjiusuo and Jilin shifan daxue lishixi 中国科学院吉林省分院歴史研究所, 吉林師範大学歴史系, ed. *Jindai Dongbei renmin geming yundong shi* 近代東北人民革命運動史 (Revolutionary movements in the modern Northeast provinces). Changchun: Jilin renmin chubanshe, 1960.

Zhongguo kexueyuan lishi yanjiusuo disan suo 中国科学院歴史研究所第三所, ed. *Xiliang yigao caogao* 錫良遺稿草稿 (Collected works of Xiliang), 2 vols. Beijing: Zhonghua shudian, 1959.

Zhongguo renmin daxue Qingshi yanjiusuo 中国人民大学清史研究所 et al., eds. *Qingdai de qidi* 清代的旗地 (Banner lands during the Qing period), 3 vols. Beijing: Zhonghua shuju, 1989.

Zhou Junshi 周君適, trans. by Zheng Ranquan 鄭然権. *Higeki no kōtei Fugi* 悲劇の皇帝溥儀 (Puyi, the tragic emperor). Kōbunsha, 1984. (Japanese translation of *Wei manzhouguo gongting mihua* 偽満洲国宮廷秘話. Chengdu: Sichuan renmin chubanshe, 1981).

Zhu Baojiong 朱保炯, and Xie Peilin 謝沛霖, ed. *Ming-Qing jinshi timing beilu suoyin* 明清進士提名碑録索引 (An index of *jinshi* names during the Ming and Qing periods), 3 vols. Shanghai: Shanghai guji chubanshe, 1963.

Index

Page numbers in *italics* refer to tables.